"Life is a great big canvas,
and you should throw all the paint you can on it."
~Danny Kaye

Published in the United States of America by
Joy Street Press
5124 East 65th Street
Indianapolis, IN 46220

First edition, July, 2014
Printed in the U.S.A.

Copyright © 2014 by Erin Jump Fry & Oriana Green
All rights reserved. No part of this publication may be reproduced except as permitted under Section 107 or 108 of the U.S. Copyright Act without prior written permission of the publisher.

Limit of Liability/Disclaimer of Warranty: While the author and publisher have employed their best efforts while preparing this book, they make no representations of warranties with respect to the accuracy or completeness of the contents and specifically disclaim any implied warranties. The advice contained herein may not be suitable for your situation. You should consult with a professional where appropriate. The author and publisher shall not be liable for any loss of profits or any other commercial damages, including but not limited to special, incidental, consequential or other damages.

Covers designed by Oriana Green

Table of Contents

Forward
Chapter One
Why You Should Take Advice From A Clown
    shifting into positivity
Chapter Two
Start With A Big Happy Day
    making time for more happiness
Chapter Three
Make Room For More Happiness In Your Life
    immersing yourself in joy
Chapter Four
What Do You Really Want?
    envisioning your big happy life
Chapter Five
Create Your Big Happy Life
    attaining your vision
Chapter Six
Enlarge Your Life
    finding support for your vision
Chapter Seven
Celebrate Your Big Happy Life
    multiplying your joy
Afterward
Happitionary

Dedication:
For all the Funsters who played with me on Happy's Place and everyone who watched at home. Your enthusiasm inspired me for eight goofy years, and I'm so glad we reconnected.

And, of course, for the next generation…my darling daughter, Ella.
Still silly and still clowning around,
Mike Fry

Foreword
By Erin Fry

Where does one start to write a prologue for a book that has been a lifetime in the making? Especially when you are just a small part of the story. Which story you might ask? The story of a Big Happy Life. This book was Mike Fry's last big project. Originally begun as a book on goal setting and how to achieve your dreams, over the years I've watched and encouraged its metamorphosis into what you have before you. By putting it into your hands, he's just checked one more life goal off his list. Thank you.

What is a story?

I believe a story is a vehicle for sharing our values and beliefs, and that story telling is only worthwhile when it tells others what we stand for. Not what we do. We need your story and what it means to us, in the world. Only you can write it and only you can tell it. That's what makes you priceless. This is one such story--the story of Mike Fry and his Big Happy Life.

Mike and I would pick this project up, work on it, put it down, mull it over. He got discouraged and would take long breaks from it. But we always had it in the back of our minds. We never stopped discussing it, and we would always come back to it. Partners on the project would come and go, each time taking the proverbial wind out of his sails. Causing him to set it aside. Until we found a friend, Oriana Green, who got the vision and was able to draw out the Big Happy Life of Mike and turn his beliefs, values and life experiences into a real physical book of Happiness (Happy-nings).

Seven years, roughly seven re-workings and we finished the project (FINALLY)! Mike's life, philosophies and zany wacky humor-filled outlook are all here. In print. Solid proof that until his death in November 2012, he Lived. Not existing day to day, playing by "the rules" or going through the motions, but really LIVING. Loud. He created a Big Happy Life. He packed his days with memorable moments, experiences and authentic interactions. He was always trying to get the laugh and add a bit more fun, humor and happiness into peoples lives. Into the world. I'm so filled with joy for the part I played in it. We definitely played...

Mike never saw the finished, edited and polished book. His birthday, October 25th, 2012 was our big reveal day, and as fate would have it, that turned out to be the day his condition deteriorated. His book, this perpetual project, once again was put back on the shelf...until now. I'm happy to now be in a place where I can pull it back out and breathe life into it once again. And no, we're not in denial about Mike being gone, but we decided to leave the book as it was written—in the present tense—because his message is still very much alive.

There wasn't a chance to give this book to Mike, but I can give it to you. He lived it. A book intended to serve as an example on how to live a richer, fuller life and how through that you can be happy. Hopefully you enjoy it. Smile. Laugh. Shed some tears and get inspired to live your one and only Big Happy Life.

Chapter One
Why You Should Take Happiness Advice From A Clown

In this chapter:
- ✓ Lessons from a clown
- ✓ Big clown shoes and bigger ideas
- ✓ No rutabagas
- ✓ What do we mean by happiness, anyway?
- ✓ Get happy, live longer
- ✓ Do you deserve to be happy?
- ✓ We're all broken…and we're all fixable
- ✓ What's your hyper happy?
- ✓ Happiness is a renewable resource
- ✓ What's your Happy Number?
- ✓ Take Your Happy Life Quiz
- ✓ What do we mean by Your **BIG** Happy Life?
- ✓ A free and easy secret of happiness
- ✓ You CAN make time for a BIG happy life
- ✓ It doesn't matter where you start
- ✓ What nonsense have you been telling yourself?
- ✓ Go the extra 3.6 miles

> "If we seek happiness first, everything else will follow."
> ~ Deepak Chopra

Why You Should Take Happiness Advice From A Clown

Short answer: Because clowns know happy. Their whole job description is to make people smile and laugh, to transform sadness. Clowns are in the joy business. (You might not think a pie in the face is funny until you get to launch one.) Most of his life people have laughed at Mike Fry. First as a class clown, then while attending Clown College and performing in Ringling Brothers Barnum & Bailey Circus. (If you think you have a shoe fetish, you should see inside Mike's closet.) That lead to eight years as the star and writer of his own nationally syndicated children's TV show, *Happy's Place*. (Anyone who truly enjoys entertaining a hundred rowdy kids for several hours every day must develop a joyful soul.) Producing his TV show, Mike also learned managerial and business skills, which allowed him to branch out into inventing toys and fantastically fun food products. Donning his silly entrepreneur's hat, Mike figured out how to integrate humor into his business life and how to create and sustain joy in his workplace. After founding several successful businesses, Mike hit the road to share what he had learned and teach others how to bring more happiness into their lives.

While Mike no longer clowns full-time, he still infuses his life with clowning around—and he'll always be a clown at heart. Besides, he performs occasionally and does public speaking on the topic of *What A Clown Can Teach You About Business*, among other things. Keep in mind, though, **this is a book on how to be happier from a clown's perspective—not a book on how to *be* a clown.**

Here are a few other reasons why you might feel like listening to a clown:

1. **Give yourself permission to be silly.** Adults don't have enough silliness in their lives. When's the last time you finger painted or wore a goofy costume or danced the limbo? When's the last time

you rolled down a grassy slope, laughing all the way as your bare feet were tickled by dandelions? How long would it take you to find a hula hoop in your home?

2. **Reconnect with happy memories from your youth or with your inner child.** You can **re**develop *eidetic perception*—which is just a fancy term for seeing the world through the eyes of a child. There are benefits to staying in touch with that aspect of yourself—like not turning into a stuffy old coot! Follow a three-year-old around for a bit and see what she sees.

3. **We can smile and laugh at the Fool, who is a stand-in for our own foibles, which we may not feel like examining.** The funniest jokes are always the ones that touch closest to home. The next time you laugh really hard at someone or something, pause and examine why you found it so funny and what that reveals about yourself.

Mike Fry has earned his Clown Wisdom, and it happily colors all aspects of his life—long after he stopped being a full-time clown. (Those who know him might say he never stopped clowning, but just changed his funny hats.)

☺ A funny hat will never go out of style; it will just look ridiculous year after year.

What's in this book (besides big clown shoes and bigger ideas)

In an increasingly challenging world, many people are reevaluating their lives, looking for meaning and fulfillment beyond tangible rewards. Perhaps you, too, have paused to see how you can improve your mood, health and wellness and find more satisfaction in your job. If so, we believe you'll find lots of ideas here to color your life in brighter shades of joy. In fact, we offer 187 ways to experience more fun and delight—we did the math so you don't have to.

Each of these seven riveting chapters presents a clownish chunk of Mike Fry's life, along with the hopefully useful lessons he learned—part scrapbook, part joy manual. Along the way we'll pause often to include you, even though we haven't met yet. We'll deliver some magical day stretchers, an emotional detox diet (no chard or kelp will be harmed) and we'll show you how to flip a day from gloom to bloom. You'll learn your personal Happy Number, how to create a Bug List and what to do with it, and how to move your personal practices into the third dimension.

Also included in this book: lots of reasons to feel better about yourself (especially after Sunday dinner with the fam, when you were asked for the umpteenth time when you're going to graduate, move out, reproduce, learn not to speak with your mouth full or _____ insert your verb here).

How do two people write one book? Oriana Green (a professional writer) began by interviewing Mike with video cameras rolling, all day long for two weeks non-stop. (Well, we did stop to indulge our strange food habits, which included blended concoctions of wildly assorted produce, microwaved yams and Voodoo Donuts.) And we're not even making that last part up. Hip residents of Portland, Oregon know what we're talking about.

Oriana is the author of many books and has a highly developed sense of fun, even though she had to work to cultivate it. At all times you can find a Frisbee and a croquet set in the trunk of her car (and she knows how to use them) so she's ready to stop, hop and play whenever the mood arises. Her loud, vibrant laugh is a distinguishing feature, and for a time she was paid by a theatre company to attend performances just to get the laughter started. The funniest thing at her house is a big green frog wind spinner which was purchased to scare voracious deer away, but actually it just makes her laugh. As a child her most treasured toy and confidante was her Bozo the Clown doll, so imagine how much fun she's having partnering with a real life clown. Oriana is also an artist, and designer. She smiles all day long as she interacts with her trusty assistant, a spoodle (spaniel/poodle) named Daffodil.

What's not in this book

☺ There are now oodles of books that scientifically dissect why people get happy, and they report their findings with zippy charts and graphs. This is not that kind of book. We do, however, share bits of sciency findings that we think won't bore you.

Also not in this book: rutabagas or pictures thereof; skunks or other things that stink up the joint; stuff to make you feel bad because your life hasn't yet turned out the way you thought it would back in high school; pleading notes from your mom; performance evaluations; lab reports; guilt trips to Whine Country; your doctor's recommendation to eat more rutabagas.

What do we mean by happiness, anyway?

While Mike finds it in bringing joy to others, and Oriana finds her utmost joy in nature, your sources may vary. Our different tastes are, indeed, what make the world go 'round in so many beautiful—and peculiar ways. **The great thing about happiness is that each of us gets to decide what it means in our own lives and pursue that.** And throughout this book we're going to help you get clarity about your own happiness formulas (or call them recipes, if you're math-averse).

Two of the Top 5 Regrets Of The Dying :
I wish I didn't work so hard.
I wish I had let myself be happier.

**"Success is getting what you want.
Happiness is wanting what you get."** ~Dale Carnegie

OUT OF MIKE'S MOUTH:
"I think happiness is something you *are*—inside and outside. To me, being a happy person means **making the most of your life every single day**. No energy? Jump some jacks. Dash around the block. Tickle a frog. (Though where you find a frog is your problem.) I think you should do everything in your power to be happy. Fun stuff, wild things, amazing activities with your family that bring you joy. Be sure your time on earth is spent with cheerful people. Teach your kids how to be happy —I'm always showing my four-year old daughter, Ella, how to be happy. I want her to experience joy every single day, and I try to instill that in her at the soul level. I say: *Honey tell me about the fun you had today, tell me what made you happy*, because I want her to learn to appreciate joy and to preserve her memories. So many people never talk about happiness—ask yourself right now: How often do you think about happiness and talk about it?

I think about happiness all the time. That's what gives energy to your life. When you're happy you're living in the moment. When you're having the best time ever, you're not noticing problems you may have—for awhile, at least, they recede to the background. Joy trumps the dumps."

"Don't waste a minute not being happy. If one window closes, run to the next window or break down a door." ~Brooke Shields

More than one flavor of happiness
Some clarity is needed here: **This book is focused on increasing your levels of deep, meaningful, enduring happiness—not the fleeting sensations that derive from pleasure.** Too much reliance on the buzz from pleasure can lead to addictions. To flourish, you must move beyond pleasure as a source of happiness. Some examples:

❋ You may believe jamoca almond fudge can make you happy, but that's a brief sugar rush from the *pleasure* of the taste. Enduring *happiness* comes from making the effort to feed yourself and family well with healthy alternatives, leaving the jamoca almond

fudge for occasional special treats, rather than daily indulgences. (Hard-earned wisdom from two reformed sugar addicts!)
* Occasionally going for a 20-minute run may give you *pleasure*, but doing that several times a week, month after month, provides the evidence that you're promoting your long term health, self-esteem and resulting *happiness*.
* Smelling the year's first lilacs causes *pleasure*; volunteering for environmental causes can make you truly *happy*.
* Getting a warm, fuzzy feeling from watching umpteen (the number that follows 4,367) videos of cute puppies brings *pleasure*, but when the cute wears off, knowing you rescued a dog who would otherwise have been needlessly killed, causes lasting happiness.

Hey, we don't have anything against pleasure—but most of us already know how to get that in our lives. And if that's *all* you have, then eventually you'll start to feel empty, because pleasure doesn't last. **Genuine happiness persists and is there to feed us daily.** Pleasure and happiness even light up different parts of our brains, but we'll save the brainy stuff for later when we'll try and impress you with quotes from neurologists and molecular biophysicists. (It'll be painless.)

Before we go any farther, **we want to say we don't believe happiness has anything to do with luck or life circumstances**. In fact, according to Harvard researcher Shawn Achor, **just 10% of your overall level of happiness is a result of your external reality. Fully 90% of your happiness level is derived from the way your brain processes the life you create for yourself by way of your experiences and your genetic makeup.** In other words, it's your attitude, your reactions and thoughts about your life that most affect how generally happy you are. That puts you firmly in charge of your own flourishing.

One of the happiest people Oriana knows spends his life in a wheelchair. He doesn't blame the drunk driver who altered his life; once he adjusted to his new reality, he's the same easy-going, cheerful guy he's always been. And Mike was certainly not dealt a cushy start in life, yet he's always been able to stroll on the sunnier side of life. If you've been blaming your poor attitude and unhappiness on bad luck—then your luck just changed—because we'll dispel that idea and show you how to create your own Big Happy Life in ways that are sustainable and immune to the irritations of daily life.

Despite beliefs in the proverbial Bluebird of Happiness, it doesn't decide to light on your shoulder and sprinkle you with joy juice—any more than it decides to poo all over your new jacket. **Happiness isn't a random event. Happiness doesn't have to be what happens to other people. Living a Big Happy Life is a CHOICE you just made by reading this book and taking action on the ideas in it!** See, you feel better already, don't you?

☺ Take a joyful leap with us—for as long as you're reading this book, suspend disbelief and accept happiness as your choice—all day, every day.

Is happiness just some fluffy idea with no real importance?

Nope. It's gratifying to see science catch up with what clowns have always known, now that the study of happiness is a bonafide serious pursuit. They even teach it at Harvard, and that's no joke. Well, maybe it's filled with jokes, but it's the truth. In fact it's the most popular class ever taught there, as it turns out most of those over-achievers are, well, very unhappy.

Close to a kajillion studies (go ahead and look it up) now confirm that **the happier you are, the healthier you are.** Spruce up your mind and your attitude and your body will display the results. Think of the chirpiest, perkiest person you know—does she also seem healthy? Statistically she (or he) is far more likely to be the picture of glowing good health. The happiest people enjoy as much as 31% more energy than Sadder Sacks. Their immune systems run like Ferraris. This is your brain on joy: if you're happy you're more apt to sleep better, eat healthier and exercise more—all of which lower your risk for heart disease, among other wretched outcomes. Though Mike occasionally played one on TV, we're not docs, so take this advice with two Jelly Belly's and watch Dr. Oz in the morning.

Study after study also shows that **the happier you are, the longer you'll probably live**. A report published by the National Academy of Sciences in November 2011, says people who claim to be the happiest live 35% longer than those who say they're the least happy. If Mopey Molly checks out at age 60 and Happy Harriet thrives until she's 80, we'll take those sunny extra 20 years, thank you very much! And we're betting you're ready to aim for that, too. Laura Kubzansky, a Harvard prof, adds: "There's a burgeoning body of work that suggests positive psychological functioning benefits health," and this study is significant because it "adds to the arsenal." The best vitamin to be a happy person is B1.

In another famous study, nuns whose writings expressed positive emotions (such as gratitude and optimism) lived seven to ten years longer than other nuns. A 2008 study by the University of Nebraska Medical Center found that happy people are generally healthier than others and often live longer. That may be because happy people see more options in life and deal with negativity and stress more effectively, researchers concluded. And the evidence is mounting to prove connections between stress and many diseases—kind of like the name implies: *dis*ease. **Which is why we're on a mission to de-stress your life.** You're welcome.

"I think patients have to keep up a good state of mind. I think most diseases start with high stress, high pressure and allowing yourself to get down." ~Dr. Burton Berkson

"I have decided to be happy, because it's good for my health." ~Voltaire

Do you deserve to be happy? Of course you do! But according to neuroscientist Gabrielle Leblanc, many people are sadly convinced it's not okay to be happy—or at least not *too* happy. That idea might come from your upbringing, your religion, or even your ethnic traditions, but however you came by it, if that's your belief, then feeling joy may cause you guilt. And that's a route to self-sabotage, which will conveniently eliminate your happiness. If there's a nagging voice in your head saying: *Who do you think you are, being jolly when so many others are* ____ (fill in the blank with your own guilt-inducing adjective) then tell that voice to go pester someone else with a less-developed sense of self-worth.

"Some people would say you shouldn't strive for personal happiness until you've taken care of everyone in the world who is starving or doesn't have adequate medical care," adds Howard Cutler, MD, co-author with the Dalai Lama of *The Art of Happiness in a Troubled World*. "The Dalai Lama believes you should pursue both simultaneously. For one thing, there is clear research showing that happy people tend to be more open to helping others. They also make better spouses and parents."

So there you go if you need them—some altruistic reasons why it's okay to be happy. Five out of four dentists agree (math isn't their specialty!): Happiness won't rot your teeth.

We're all broken…and we're all fixable

No matter how much your life has resembled a Hallmark commercial, it's clear that we all become broken in some ways. (Or at the very least we skin our emotional knees…that's a surprise, isn't it… that your emotions could have knees?) **It's what coping methods we choose to heal ourselves that can define our lives.** Did you pick alcohol, drugs, food, sex, fame, greed, ambition, ping pong, black sheepism, parenthood? Are you surprised to see parenthood on the list? Lots of parents try to compensate for their own unfulfilling childhoods by offering the world to their offspring. Similarly, some parents resurrect their own dashed dreams and saddle their tots with tiaras in an impossible quest for vicarious happiness. **But happiness can't be found out there—it must begin within.**

A better route might be to accept what's broken in our lives and examine those points for opportunities to grow. For example:
- ✸ Daddy didn't ever approve of you? Try approving more of yourself, really make a study of self-love. Write a list of 100 reasons why you are infinitely lovable. Then another 100.
- ✸ You've sublimated all your dreams to bolster someone else's. Gently bring your own desires back to life—we all deserve and need to have aspirations. It's too late to be a ballerina? It's never too late for zumba.
- ✸ You tell yourself the reason you keep job hopping is that no one appreciates you. Well, how do *you* appreciate yourself? What have you done for yourself lately? What would being truly appreciated feel like? Give that to yourself.
- ✸ Along with much of America, you've gained more weight than you ever imagined you might. Food has become both your beloved and your enemy. You think chocolate cake holds the key to perpetual happiness. Instead ask: What other kinds of sweetness are lacking in your life? Are you longing for kindness? Where else can you find comfort besides a bowl of mac 'n cheese? How else could you nurture yourself?

"We walk in the world as if we were broken, but really, everything we have is more than enough." ~Helen Wang

"Every man dies. Not every man really lives."
~William Wallace

High-flying happy hoopla

As we continue to define happiness, it helps to look backward. Start thinking about your own hyper happy experiences (that don't involve Duncan Hines or Ben and Jerry). Are there any common threads? Which ones continue to give you warm fuzzies? For Mike, it was easy to pick his fave:

MIKE KEEPS TALKING:
"**One of the happiest days of my life was certainly my wedding.** I waited a long time to find somebody, because I didn't want to settle or be like some of my friends who were on their third marriages while still in their 20s. When I met Erin, she was considerably younger, and that concerned me for awhile. Then I met someone by chance who told me his story of falling in love with a younger woman and how he let his friends talk him out of the romance. Six years later, he still thought about her every day. His story convinced me I didn't want to regret my choice, and I needed to pursue this amazing woman I'd met.

We had everything in common, we had fun all the time, we were very spontaneous, and I knew I HAD to marry someone who was spontaneous. So I went down on one knee and asked Erin to marry me and she said *Yes*! I was getting ready to fly to Asia to do some speaking, so I blurted: "Why don't you come with me and let's get married in Thailand?" And she's like: *When?* And I said: "In a week." And bless her heart she agreed. So suddenly we're on a plane to Thailand, we had nothing planned, we had no wedding clothes or anything. But we had friends there who stood up for us, and they helped pull together a wedding on the beach at sunset. In Thailand you can have beautiful clothes made quickly, so we got fitted one day and married the next. We had about seventy-five friends from nine countries there, and it all came together easily and spontaneously. It was fabruous and a truly magical time."

☺ You can't *make* someone else happy (nor can anyone else make you happy). You can, however, enjoy being **in happiness** together.

**"When you do things from your soul,
you feel a river running through you, a joy." ~Rumi**

Happiness is a renewable resource

Sure, happiness is never permanent—what begins as a great day can suddenly turn into a bad episode of *Father Doesn't Know Squat*. Our goal is to give you the insights and tools to be able to **renew your happiness under just about any circumstance:** everything from a flat tire to getting fired. Yes, sometimes life deals us tragedies that are truly devastating. And yet, eventually most people recover enough to carry on. It may be a very different life than what you were enjoying, but it's still your precious *life,* and no matter how much you may be grieving or healing, you deserve to recover some level of joy in your life. **Here are a few tips to help you return to happiness:**

* **Watch for tiny signs of positive change:** a subtle shift in your mood, time that passes without sadness, an urge to be productive again, catching yourself smiling or even laughing at your daughter's silly joke. Notice and applaud these shifts.

☺ What do you get when you cross a parrot with a hyena?
An animal that laughs at its own jokes.

* **Journal about those small increments of change and identify any patterns you can repeat.** Do certain TV programs lift your spirits? Does going for a run in a certain location cheer you up? When you confide in close friends do you feel better? Is there a park you enjoy? Go there more often. Once you spot positive patterns, do more of those things. Conversely, do fewer of the things that you notice drag you down.
* **Get moving again.** It's a fact (you can look it up!) that changing your physical situation helps change your mood. Go for a walk, even if it's just around the block. Lose yourself in cleaning or organizing—tackling some project you never have time for can be enormously satisfying on a basic level. (Yes, Virginia, there is another sort of joy to be found within your refrigerator, in a

sparkling vegetable crisper.) Do some gardening—offer to help someone else if you don't have your own. Digging in the dirt can pay great emotional dividends as you reconnect viscerally with the earth.

☺ Time: Don't spend it all in one place.

- **Pamper yourself.** After you ruin your nails pulling up crabgrass, treat yourself to a spa day. Or if you're a guy who thinks real men don't get mani-pedis, then go golfing, mountain biking, power tool browsing or whatever manly pursuit makes you smile.
- **This tip comes with a guarantee:** find a park with adult-sized swings and treat yourself to ten minutes of swinging as high as you possibly can. Repeat to yourself (silently or aloud) some variation on this: *I am rising above my situation…I leave my troubles beneath me…I am light, I am free.* Rinse and repeat daily. Anchoring affirmations with relevant actions deepens their effect.
- **Devise simple delights.** Crawl out of the cave! Even lunch with a friend or a movie night with your sister can be enough of a treat to stir your soul and start your joy on an upward trajectory. But don't stop there—keep adding ever more exciting activities to your calendar, until you're able to return to a fully functional social life. It might take a year to get there, but savoring future delights delivers happiness in the process.

"When we give our story to the world, we celebrate our common humanity. We create safe spaces for others to have their pain lifted off of them. And when we do that, we create happiness."
~Helen Wang

"Happiness is realizing that if we were all to throw our problems onto a table, most of us would take our own back!" ~Dr. Happy

And baby makes wheeee!
MIKE KEEPS TALKING:
"About a year or so after we got married we had a beautiful little daughter, **Ella**. The great thing about her is she's just so much fun. A lot of people ask if she's always so happy, and she is—she's always giggling and having a good time. I love the fact that she's a happy child. I always hoped I'd have a daughter who's happy and fun. So the day I found out Erin was pregnant, I decided I was going tell my child—while she was in the womb—all the things I wanted her to be. Every day I put my hands around my wife and sang a little song to Ella, even though I don't have a good singing voice. This is what I sang:

Happy baby, happy happy baby. You like to laugh and you like to smile. You're so happy in every single way.

And I would do that every day, because I wanted her to hear that and sense that, and there are studies which suggest that may be possible. And then I'd put my head on my wife's stomach and tell Ella my hopes for her. Things like:

You're so creative, you're the most creative little girl ever. You are so, so smart...you learn so fast. And you are the happiest girl...you giggle all the time. And you love to meet people...it's easy for you to meet people. You are super positive, which is so important in life, because then people want to be around you. And you love to share.

And I can tell you that it makes me feel good, because at age 4 Ella really is that little girl now. And that's what I continue to hope for my daughter—to always be a happy child."

Where are you on the Joy Scale right this minute?
In our experience, happiness isn't a result, a permanent goal or an end game, but rather a continuum, and all we can do is move along it and aim toward happiER. **Pick your number from this chart—whatever represents how you feel right this minute.** Your **Happy Number** will be our shorthand throughout this book and can also be a

useful way of measuring and tracking your happiness. Whatever that number is, we believe it will surely rise as you read these stories and implement the suggestions we have for amplifying the joy in your life.

00: no joy in sight
05: grieving
10: depressed
15: really sad
20: down in the dumps
25: drained, blah
30: neutral
35: just contented
40: growing optimism, glimmers of joy
45: feeling positive
50: hopeful, upbeat
55: anticipating goodness, joy is rising
60: enjoying this moment here, now
65: quite happy, all is well
70: laughing, having a blast
75: playing
80: really, really happy
85: feels like a vacation
90: feel like dancing (or skipping or singing or leaping)
95: on top of the world
100: pure bliss

You get to assign meaning to your number, but here are some guidelines:
- If you study the chart, you'll see the **bottom third** denotes moods which are sub-optimal. Of course everyone has a wide range of moods, and we all have our blue days and times when we're just too exhausted to be aware of much joy in our lives.

- The **middle third** shows improving conditions and is a fine place to spend time.
- The **top third** of the chart is where life really sings and zings and where you sport a lilt in your voice and a perpetual high in your heart. This is where we prefer to live as much of our lives as possible.

It's not realistic to write about happiness without mentioning UNhappiness. Try tracking your moods for a week or so in writing. If you find you're spending more time than you'd like in the lower region of the Joy Scale, then by identifying all the things which are causing you unhappiness, you can begin to address what needs altering and start to rise up the scale. Amazingly, even people who are aware they're unsatisfied with their life rarely stop to take a full inventory of their situation—nor do most people plan systematic changes to reverse the situation. But that's not you, is it? **You're reading this book, because on some level you're ready to open yourself to more joy.** So hang on and say *ahhhhhhh*! Louder…we can't hear you. That's better. For our mutual convenience we're going to pretend we heard you.

☺Happiness can be found all around you, but you must train your eyes to see it and your heart to open to it. Some people cause happiness **wherever** they go. Others **whenever** they go. Which are you? Try creating a simple **Joy Tracker Chart** to track your own joy. Get out a ruler, reward yourself with silly stickers to visually express your joy level each and every day. Make it part of your journal. Live it!

> **"I'd like to be as optimistic as my dog, who believes that every knock on the door is for him."** ~Every Dogowner

What do we mean by your BIG happy life?
MORE MIKE:
"When I say a BIG LIFE, I'm not talking about living in the biggest house, or having a big bank account or driving the fastest, biggest car. I'm talking about living in a *way* that's big and exciting. Anyone can do that, no matter what your finances are. You can live a life that's larger right now, that's full of more happiness. I think of it as electrifying my life. More juice. More zip. More zap. More buzz. It's about expecting the most of myself in all ways. **For me, it includes making each day as full of fun as possible.**"

Savor some *fun du jour*:
- ☺How about an early morning walk at dawn before your neighborhood springs to noisy life? What a great time to **select** the tone and mood *you* want to enjoy during your day.
- ☺Surprise your Honey with breakfast in bed just because it's Tuesday, and maybe even put some effort into it! Waffles with homemade berry syrup would be nice, thankyouverymuch.
- ☺Wear something extra colorful, fun or unexpected. Pin a flower to your lapel. Declare it's Wacky Hat Day.
- ☺Grab a co-worker and toss around a Frisbee at lunchtime. (A park would probably be nicer than your conference room.)
- ☺Send a friend a snazzy e-card just to say: *I'm thinking of you*. Or: *You tickle me*. Or: *I'll tickle you*.
- ☺Offer to help someone, even if at first it feels like an inconvenience. (That will wear off.)
- ☺Bring treats for your co-workers. They could even be *healthy* ones —what a concept! A jug of fresh cider, a bowl of fresh berries, some bags of veggie chips. Okay, sometimes you can't beat a box of decadent dipped donuts with sprinkles.
- ☺Remember people's birthdays and special anniversaries. (There's an app for that.) You don't have to spend big to create a big impression. Balloons make everything better.

Those suggestions are low to no cost at all. It's about adopting an attitude that ensures there are moments of fun in every day. Why on earth wouldn't you want to do that? You don't want to live a dull, boring, same-old-same-old life do you? We didn't think so! Our goal is to help you live an extraordinary life, one that's miles above average, one that has you dancing in the streets (or at least in your living room). Or even dancing in the streets with balloons and donuts while wearing a wacky hat.

> "You can't have everything…where would you put it?"
> ~Steven Wright

> "If you ask me what I came into this world to do, I will tell you. I came to live out loud." ~Emile Zola

Pop goes the quiz
　　　Here's a simple quiz to evaluate your overall current situation.
Your Happy Life Quiz
1. How happy were you yesterday?
2. What's the overall status of your emotional life in the last six months or so? Most of the time are you generally positive in your outlook on life?
3. How satisfied are you with your life as a whole, considering other aspects of your life: relationships and family, health, career, time to relax, time to pursue your own creative ideas?
4. Do you believe your life has meaning and a clear purpose? How would you rate that aspect of your life right now?
5. Imagine the best possible life that you can for yourself—how does your current life compare?

Now add 'em up and multiply your result by two. On a scale of one to a hundred, that's your Happy Life Number. As before, we aren't going to grade your quiz by attempting to tell you what your number means—only you can decide that. (Though if it's 100, we suggest you set this book down and go jump for joy on the nearest trampoline. In fact, just pass this book on to someone who actually needs it!) While the earlier **Joy Scale** exercise revealed how you were feeling at that moment, **Your Happy Life Quiz** shows the bigger picture. Of course, if for some reason you were unusually *unhappy* when you took the quiz, that might affect it. If you feel your result is off, take it again in a few days.

Add this **Happy Life Number** to your **Joy Tracker Chart** so you can follow it, too, over time. These simple measurements can help determine how much higher you want to aim and the effort you'd like to expend.

☺ **Here's some good news:** There really is gold in them thar years! Contrary to earlier beliefs, it now appears that older adults are happier than ever, claiming their advancing age allows them to find happiness in just about anything. Turns out there really is something to the mellowing process. So even if you're a bit deficient in optimism at the moment, or even if you're sandwiched between your kids' and your parents' needs, your life really ought to improve as you age. **Sixty is the new happy!**

MIKE CONTINUES:

"I think you should do everything in life as BIG as possible, be remarkable and make every day dazzle. To lead a big, fun, awesome, happy life, I do things that have an impact, things that are big that people will remember. Go places that'll be memorable and have a big effect on your life…push your boundaries…challenge yourself to go farther. When you're stretching yourself, that's when life gets exciting. Take chances, dare to do things others won't. You can't be worried about what other people think, or what other people do—you need to create your big life on your own terms and live it full tilt. **You want to lead a big, happy life, because that's what everyone else is AFRAID to do!**

They're afraid to step forward and say to the world: *This is who I am, this is where my passion is, what I want and where I'm going. This is how I choose to live my life right now!* You really CAN create a more exciting life for yourself. I'm not saying every day has to be thrill packed, but I like to always have:
- big goals in motion
- big trips on the horizon that I'm preparing for
- great books on hand to keep sparking new ideas
- something fun and surprising in the works for my family

There's another BIG reason why I like to have lots of activities and projects in various stages of completion, and it's **a great Secret of Happiness: ANTICIPATION can deliver a huge dose of fun and joy."**

Think about how much fun it is to plan even a simple surprise for someone, or to find the perfect gift for a friend's birthday. (Brenda still treasures that sasquatch T-shirt.) Recall how much delight you felt thinking ahead to the moment of revelation. Often the research and preparing for a major trip can be nearly as exciting as the taking of it. In fact, **just planning for a vacation can make you feel good**. A 2010 Dutch study revealed that anticipating a future trip upped people's happiness for as much as eight weeks *before* the actual event.

Learn to slow down and savor each stage of a project, not just the completion. **It's the quality of the experiences you have while *doing* the project that add up to a big life.** Have an important date or event to go to? Luxuriate in the preparations, in honoring your body and creating the right mindset for the interaction. Turn off your cell phone and arrive centered and focused and ready to be fully present for the experience to unfold. Look for joyful moments and seek out the happiest people in the room.

Happit: *anticipating* No, that's not a typo…we just crunched "happy habit" and got *happit*, which feels more fun and less tiresome to achieve.

Every day for the next 21 days find something to anticipate, even if it's just leaving work a bit early or having something special for dinner. Do try though to schedule some longer term activities, so you can practice anticipating them again and again. Lavish some time on this—that's the whole point—the time you spend in delicious anticipation IS the joyful payoff.

Why 21 days? because another Harvard whiz determined that **it only takes 21 days of consistently doing something new to make it a habit for life.** After 21 days your shiny new happits will become automatic—how glad-making is that? Let's hear a whoop of joy for that one. The operative word in the formula is *consistently*—**if you skip a day you have to start over**—so set up a tracking system of some sort to help you attain that goal on your first go-around.

As with most of the happits you'll find here (which are all collected at the very end of the book for your enjoyment), you'll be way more apt to stay with them if you write them down and track them. You're going to hear this more than once from us, so get over it: **there is no way to overstate the immense value of journaling**. Both Mike and Oriana are lifelong journalers and have found infinite joy and value in revisiting their notebooks. Journals act as time capsules so you can see the person you used to be—and appreciate the person you've become. You don't have to be a "writer"—this is not about creating literature, it's about preserving key facets of your life and recording the trajectory of it. Besides, you'll be amazed how useful journaling can be when you have a problem to solve. Writing out your thoughts can really help sort out your priorities and guide you toward resolutions. Besides, putting your thoughts on paper is a proven mood shifter. ***Just do it!***

☺**Happy Hour:** (Which in our book can be any hour of the day or night, but has nothing to do with cocktails—unless of course you want it to.) In our version, you spend some quality time capturing daily happiness by recording the best moments in a fun book. You might write, sketch, paste a photo or movie ticket stub—whatever preserves the memory for you. The best part is that when you need a boost you can browse through happier days and relive those highlights—kind of like rehydrating dried apples, but without the sugar spike.

> **"The purpose of life is the expansion of happiness. Happiness is the goal of every other goal." ~ Deepak Chopra**

You CAN make time for a BIG happy life

We all need some relaxation time, so we're not saying you shouldn't enjoy your free time, but you can make *some* of your free time really pay off big-time. Time for passion projects, for implementing your big ideas. Whatever your distraction device is—*The Housewives of Hoboken*, video games, gambling, mindless internet surfing, fiction, shopping, Angry Aardvarks—ask yourself how much time you *want* to devote to distraction each week. Now ask yourself how much time you *actually* spend on your distractions each week. **A lot of happiness can be found in the difference between those two numbers.** For the mathematically inclined, it looks like this: **Distracting activities – reasonable relaxation time = found time to focus on a bigger life.**

It really is that simple. The trick is to catch yourself at the moments of choice and realize you are making a conscious choice to spend your time in a potentially wasteful way. One proven tactic is to make it easier to do the healthy thing through preparation (have all the materials you need for your project all organized ahead of time). Conversely, **make it tougher to choose the lesser alternative by creating small obstacles like these:**

- ☼ Try taping a bright note to your gaming controls or TV remote: *Is this the best use of my time?*
- ☼ Tape or place a large sign over the TV screen that you have to physically move in order to watch: *How will this help me create a big, happy life?*

- ☼ Keep your credit cards frozen in a block of ice with a note: Do I really need to buy something today? Is this retail therapy or a necessity?
- ☼ Tape a note to your steering wheel: *Am I driving myself crazy or driving myself toward joy today? What mood do I want to be in as I travel and when I arrive at my destination? Choose that one!*
- ☼ Install wallpaper on your computers, phones, tablets, etc. that reinforces what your true values are, what you actually want to get out of life. Take time to study it every time you use your device, so you're forced to consider if the activity you have in mind supports this vision for your life.

It isn't that you need to stop yourself from ever doing relaxing, diverting activities again, but rather that *ideally*, each time you do engage in them, it's because you've weighed all the options for your valuable time and made a conscious decision to be distracted. Again, we're not against entertaining activities as long as you also make space in your life for things that might matter more. **Every waking moment is an opportunity to make a better choice.** That's a LOT of opportunity packed into each day!

Happit: *finding time* Every day for those magical 21 days, consciously change your behavior, and instead of doing some distracting activity, spend at least ten minutes thinking about your happiness level and what you might do to improve it. You might spend the time with your Joy Tracker chart or yes—journaling. (*We warned you we'd nag you about this!*) For bonus points, track how much extra time you gather and put to better use.

☺ Turn off any self-talk that says you're destined to live a small life. You're not. (Or an unhappy life either!)

It doesn't matter where you start, it matters where you finish

Mike overcame quite a few challenges as a kid, and the actions he took to thrive in spite of them pointed him toward the study of positive thinking and happiness.

MIKE REMEMBERS:

"If you'd been able to observe me as a young child, you wouldn't have thought: *This kid will turn out to be a Happiness Teacher*. Growing up in rural Indiana, I knew what is was to be poor. There were times when I had to sleep in a bathtub. I remember hunting around the house for 20 cents to buy a loaf of bread. My dad became disabled from lead poisoning he got from working in a paint factory, so there was lots of economic uncertainty.

I was massively afraid of the dark from about age 7 to 12. I only realized a few years ago that it was probably caused by watching an episode of the *Twilight Zone,* which scared the holy crap out of me. Like many kids, I was looking at TV for an alternate reality to offset my current life, but the one I found in that show didn't help.

All through grade school I struggled with a speech impediment—I couldn't say R or S—and every Tuesday I got called out of class for speech therapy. Of course the other kids were unmerciful in their teasing, which only fueled my desire to overcome the problem. By continuing to practice on my own at home, by sixth grade I was the only one in my school who succeeded in correcting my speech.

I agree with the scientists who say about half our happiness level is genetically determined, because despite those childhood disadvantages, **this is how I managed to maintain a sunny outlook on life:**

★ I always focused on the best possible scenario, not the worst case.
★ I didn't dwell on being poor or on the problems my family faced.
★ I learned to be my own champion and stick up for myself.
★ I suppose my innate sense of humor helped me cope, too."

☺ How about you? Is your cuppa joy half empty or half full? As Earl Nightingale pointed out: "Our attitude toward life determines life's attitude towards us." Even the most cynical person can find ways to be more positive if the desire is there. No one is born a negative thinker—it was learned along the way—so decide to UNlearn it. You **can** reframe that sour, dour view. Try this experiment: consciously *look* for positive ideas, experiences, signs and people throughout your day. It sure beats looking for dust bunnies under the bed.

> "The pessimist sees difficulty in every opportunity.
> The optimist sees opportunity in every difficulty."
> ~Winston Churchill

One really big advantage for Mike was that he just naturally thought in affirmations—he just knew how to be his own cheerleader. (Being double jointed helps.) As kind of a scrawny kid and not very worldly, he read biographies of two men who greatly inspired him. Bruce Lee, the ultimate martial arts master and philosopher, and long before he got political, bodybuilder Arnold Schwarzenegger. Both men were outsiders who achieved worldwide success, and both men had reached their heights through sheer determination, focus and grit. Both overcame hardships, which gave Mike a lot of hope as a country kid who had yet to even make it out of Indiana. Their accomplishments gave him a sense of what was possible for his own life. As a result, he began training his mind along with his body with simple affirmations like these:

- ✤ **I am invincible, I am as strong as a tree**
- ✤ **I'm as agile as a cat**
- ✤ **I'm a winner, I will succeed**
- ✤ **I study everything around me and am constantly learning valuable things**

Since he was able to see results from his positive thinking experiments, he was inspired to search for teachers who knew more about how to harness that ability. **Self-talk is always going on, so it might as well be positive!** But if you'd been able to observe his life when he was a young child, you might have thought: *This kid will never amount to anything, will never grow beyond his humble roots.*

MORE FROM MIKE:

"Things started to improve when I first realized I was funny. I probably figured it out in seventh grade, when the teacher asked a question about Indians. Before I knew it, I had everyone laughing hysterically, and I thought—*wow*—*I must be a funny guy*. I was always a wild, radical kid, but until then I didn't realize I could make the whole class respond to me. Looking around at everyone laughing, **I realized what a great feeling it was to be the source of that much happiness.**

As the class clown, I never had an idea I didn't try. One day I brought my unicycle to high school, and in a crowded hall I hopped on it and zoomed around as fast as I could, flying along until some teachers happened by who didn't appreciate my skill. Even though I could finally pronounce it, I didn't feel much remorse.

In middle school, the way I was rewarded for being a jokester was by having my name announced over the speaker system several times a week: *Mike Fry, please report to the office.* And then I'd have to go see the principal, who proceeded to paddle me for whatever nonsense I'd been up to—I was the boy who never met a dare he didn't like. **So I started out getting punished for what eventually became my career—making people laugh.** (Insert irony here.) I remember my teachers saying to me in a demeaning way: *"So, you think you're a comedian, Fry?"* And I was already thinking to myself: *Yeah, I'm going to be one someday.* **So what other people viewed as a fault, I turned into an asset—it was a shift of perception.** For me it was about having fun, entertaining the other kids and not taking everything so seriously. I

learned to NEVER believe the limits other people try to force on me."

- Mike's teachers saw a screw-up who'd never amount to anything because he didn't apply himself in math (or English or history or anything they deemed important).
- Mike saw himself as someone who had natural talents which could be developed into a career.

How many people do you suppose never followed their dreams, because they *did* believe the negative things they were told? Way too many, no doubt. Mike says he never worries about what other people are going to think—that's his job as a clown or a comedian: to take the risk to fall flat on his face. **But therein lies the laughter.** (Of course it helps to know where the banana peels are!)

"Never, and I mean never, allow anyone else's ideas of who you can or can't become sully your dream or pollute your imagination. This is your territory, and a KEEP OUT sign is a great thing to erect at all entrances to your imagination." ~Wayne Dyer

A college for clowns—who knew?

It's sort of a fluke that Mike Fry ended up in the circus, because when he was a kid he never even got to go to one. The first time he saw a circus was on TV, watching a *60 Minutes* segment on Ringling Brothers Clown College. As a young teen he learned that every year about 5,000 people tried out for the college, and sixty were chosen to attend. Then half of those might join the actual circus. By that point in Mike's life, his barely legible left-handed writing was already on his wall: academics were not his strong suit, and he'd already decided to pursue a career in entertainment. So the idea of going away to a special college to learn to clown around sounded like his chance to join Phi Beta *Cappa*.

MIKE CONTINUES:

"Besides being funny, something else I knew I was good at was physical skills like juggling and gymnastics. Football, basketball, all the team sports, didn't appeal to me the way developing my individual skills did. Clown College just seemed like the coolest place for me to try and get into. **But I knew I needed a plan.**

At age 15 I decided I absolutely wanted to defeat the odds and get chosen, so I started on a program of physical training. I was hyper-focused and went to the gym all the time and taught myself gymnastics. I became obsessed with walking on my hands—going all the way down the gym floor and then walking backwards all the way back.

I taught myself to juggle by reading a library book. The author, Carlo, explained how to make juggling clubs out of bleach bottles, and I began to practice juggling night and day. Then I advanced to juggling balls from the toy store. Keep in mind this was in the dark, dark ages, way before YouTube made this something 4-year-old Ukrainian donkeys could learn.

My Dad was always a big believer in giving 110% to anything you really cared about, so I learned that from him and took it to heart."

On Friday nights when other kids were out partying, Mike went to the Huntington College gym to work on learning new skills. He watched their cheerleaders and tried to imitate their tumbling skills. **Mike was as dedicated as any athlete in training, it's just that his sport was laughter.** There was a lot of trial. And even more error. But he did everything he could think of to prepare for whatever he might be asked to do in the circus:
- He climbed ropes to develop upper body strength.
- He learned dangerous trampoline tricks.
- He taught himself to do diving stunts, which he admits was scary.

Basically, he sacrificed his entire high school social life to prepare for this one shot at joining the Greatest Show on Earth.

It's kind of amazing, since he'd never even been to a circus and didn't really know what clowns did! Nor was there anyone to coach him. No one in his small town had any idea how to prepare for something like that, so he had to rely on his own instincts. While his classmates were focused on earning good grades to get into great colleges, Mike was devising crazy stunts to get into Clown College. For him, that really was his Harvard. He knew he wasn't college bound in the traditional way, so he had to make the most of this one opportunity. He likens it to trying out for *American Idol* today. The odds are really stacked against you, but if you have talent and you stay focused, you just might make it. Though there was certainly sacrifice involved, Mike also had plenty of fun training for his big audition—mostly because he was training with *intent*.

What special skills do you have & have you developed them? You might want to spend some time contemplating what goals you've had—or still have—that might inspire you with that degree of passion and commitment.

☺ **What's your passion project?** Write the Great American Zombie Romance? Sail to Bora Bora and back? Climb Mt. Diggetydoo? Open a chandlery for other people sailing to Bora Bora? Learn to cook like an Iron Chef? Brew artisanal pear cider for Iron Chefs? Export yourself to Honduras and import handmade hammocks? **Having a BIG dream heats up your life.** Go even bigger and aim for a **BHAG**: a **Big Hairy Audacious Goal.** Just because you're currently doing something important from 9 to 5 every day doesn't mean the ship to Bora Bora has sailed without you. (Okay, the 2:53 from Lahaina has left the dock, but there'll be another one. Your job now is to get your seafaring behind on another boat.) We'll show you the way to the dock.

Go the extra 3.6 miles when applying for anything

After high school Mike was ready to go for his dream. When he received his application for Clown College, he devoted three days to filling it out. Though he didn't realize it at the time, it was meant to be a psychological evaluation of sorts, and he was quite amazed at the kind of questions they asked, including:
- What makes you laugh?
- Do your friends laugh at you?
- Are you really funny?
- Are you afraid of small places?
- What makes you cry?
- What kind of people do you like to be around?
- Are there any kinds of people who make you nervous?
- Would you like to go around the world?

So he decided to fill it out from the perspective of being funny. Then instead of just mailing it back like most people did, **he decided to really try and stand out from those 5,000 other applicants.** So he had a buddy follow him around and film him with a Super 8 camera, performing all the skills he'd worked so hard the last three years to develop. He did Frisbee tricks, acrobatic diving, freestyle skateboard stunts. He wanted to become an acrobat on a skateboard—he could ride a quarter of a mile doing a handstand on a skateboard. In sending Ringling Brothers a film, Mike wanted them to see that he was innovative by doing something they hadn't asked him to do, something which would really showcase his skills.

Have you ever wanted something that badly? What did you do about it? How about now…can you imagine something you want to apply that much dedication toward? We'll come back to this, but we wanted to set the cogs in the recesses of your mind turning.

But why clowning as a profession?
MIKE EXPLAINS:

"I wanted to become a clown because I loved to make people laugh. It wasn't that I liked it, I LOVED it. It brought me a lot of energy, and it gave me a lot of passion for what I wanted to do. The response was immediate and the gratification was instantaneous. I think that's something all comedians and clowns share…they crave the immediate feedback from an audience. Clowning seemed like a perfect fit for the joy I found in physical skills combined with silly stunts designed to evoke laughter."

☺ **Job description of a clown:** Take pie in face. Wipe away cream. Smile through it all. Is that so different from your job?

They're not laughing *at* me if I'm doing it on purpose; rather, they're laughing because *I want them to laugh*.

Three rings calling
MIKE REMEMBERS:
"The happiest day of my life with the circus was the day I got the call. The guy on the phone sounded so serious that I thought he was going to turn me down. I'm sure they'd never gotten an application like mine. He asked me to tell them why I sent in a film of my skills. Finally he goes: 'Well Mike, based on those answers, we've selected you to be one of the sixty people chosen to attend Clown College at Ringling Brothers winter quarters in Venice, Florida.' As soon as I hung up I was screaming and jumping around the room and hugging my mom. My parents were excited for me and 1000% supportive. They always told me they didn't care what I did as long as I was happy."

Even though Mike figured out early in life how to be happy—which helped him reach a major dream at a young age and go on to have other life successes—**it's never too late to learn how to create your own BIG happy life**. Even if you believe your window of opportunity has been painted shut, you can still pry it open with the tools we have for you here. Don't ever give up on yourself or your dreams…some version of them can always be brought to life. It's never too late to be happy… you could select *chirpy* from the mood menu right this second.

AFFIRMATIONS: I am willing to do whatever it takes to create a big happy life for myself. I am open to joy in every form.

☺ The early bird might get the worm, but the second mouse gets the cheese.

In the next chapter…
We provide quick, fast, safe, reliable, effective, low-fat, low-carbohydrate, low-carbon emission ways to add more happiness to your days. These methods are all-green—chartreuse even!—and no wheat grass was harmed in the making of these tips.

Chapter Two
Start With A Big Happy Day

In this chapter:
- ✓ Shut your eyes
- ✓ Get into slo-mo
- ✓ Start your day as a C.L.O.W.N.
- ✓ Lunch Launch: finding 150 minutes a week or more
- ✓ Listmania
- ✓ Take a break for repair work
- ✓ Unsentencing your commute
- ✓ Make dinner a winner by making a shift
- ✓ How hard will you push?
- ✓ Have a Hot Nudge Sunday (no, it's not what you think)
- ✓ Sweet dreams

Of course, your big happy life is created one day at a time. So let's start today. *What do you mean you're not ready yet?* Would you rather waste more days of your precious life wallowing in negativity, depression or plain brown paper boredom? *All righty then. That's more like it!* We'll get back to Mike's big adventures in a bit, but what we have to share with you now is too important to wait even one more chapter. Of course your mileage may vary, but these are some of our **best tips for squeezing maximum happiness out of every day**, plus we'll show you **how to find more quality time in your day**, and that's no joke. While we don't expect you'll implement all these ideas—at least not all at once—we do hope you'll test drive most of them to see how they might fit into your life. Okay, assuming you begin your days in the morning, let's start there. (If you're a shift worker with an irregular schedule, then heaven help you…read up on what sleep experts have to say about how that impacts your health, weight, mood, Twinkie consumption and overall well-being.) Everybody else, rise and shine!

Don't get up yet

As soon as you open your eyes, slam 'em back shut until you tell yourself these three things:
1. Today I choose to feel as much joy as I can hold.
2. Today I spill my excess joy over others.
3. Today is already a good day.

> **"Time is a created thing.**
> **To say: *I don't have time* is to say: *I don't want it.*" ~Lao Tzu**

Break|fast Slow|fix

Though it may seem counter-intuitive when you're rushed with morning madness, pausing to get centered, to take a few deep breaths, to be certain you have everything you need for your day, can actually get your day off to a better start than racing around like a gerbil on a wheel going nowhere fast. For a more advanced experience of this, build in

5-10 minutes of high quality peace by meditating or doing a bit of yoga or any sort of stretching. Perhaps it's adding five minutes so you can really relax in your shower and let the hot water pound your shoulders into submission, or getting up before anyone else to savor pure quiet even for a few minutes. **When you're rushing around things rarely go well:** you fail to eat a good breakfast; you forget to bring your lunch/laptop/gym bag/optimistic self with you. You lose patience with your Pomeranian when she won't poop on schedule; you forget to take cupcakes to your third grader's classroom—or worse, you forget to take your third grader to her classroom. Fifteen minutes less sleep is a fair trade-off to start your day less frantically.

Happit: *slowing* Try this every day for 21 days before you dismiss the idea. You might be amazed at the impact a few extra minutes can make. Get up 10-15 minutes earlier and plan ahead how to use the time well.

> "It's not so much how busy you are, but *why* you are busy. The bee is praised; the mosquito is swatted." ~Marie O'Conner

> "Sometimes I have believed as many as six impossible things before breakfast." ~Lewis Carroll

Try this: Start your day as a C.L.O.W.N. (No greasepaint needed.)
C = Choose
The most important thing you can do each morning is choose your intentions for the day. Most people just allow themselves to get swept up into other people's needs and wants and fall into routine patterns of response: buckwheat waffles—*sure*; ham sandwich—*okay*; new crayons—*in your backpack*; AA batteries—*put them on my list*; rubber chicken—*where you always keep it*. They get pulled in unexpected directions, often spending their time in ways that aren't really productive or self-nurturing. (*Why do I have to hunt for your rubber chicken again!*) Then at the end of the day, they wonder why they're so tired, why all they feel

like doing is numbing out with some industrial-strength, high-carb discomfort food.

Instead, try devoting a few minutes each morning to questions like these:
- ✦ Who do you want to be today? Someone everyone turns to for help and encouragement or the Office Whiner? The Good Deed Doer? The Expert? The Recluse who takes great care of herself?
- ✦ How will you create balance in your life today?
- ✦ What emotional tone do you want to set for your day?

Guess what—YOU get to determine all this for yourself, every day of your life. These are all CHOICES you get to make. Cool, huh? We think so. And hey, it's free to give it a whirl. No exotic equipment required, just your open and willing mind. (We know you have that or you wouldn't be reading this book.) **Choosing the tone for your day is very empowering, and that's a direct path to more happiness in your life.**

"Are you whining about a painful yesterday, or preparing for a joyful today? Your choice will determine your day."
~M. Williamson tweet

L = Laugh

What will you do for fun today? When? If you don't schedule it, it probably won't happen. How big a priority is it? Do you really mean that? Cross your heart and hope to try? Maybe you could watch that ridiculous YouTube clip everyone is talking about. Or read a funny book. Or visit a humor website. Laughter doesn't actually release endorphins, says psychologist Steven Sultanoff, Ph.D., an expert on therapeutic humor. However, it does increase your heart rate and activate your muscular system, making you feel instantly revived. Even more important, a hearty belly laugh provides what Sultanoff calls a **cognitive shift**. "Energy levels are directly related to the way people think," he says. "And humor changes thought patterns in ways that are very uplifting." So make time to tickle your funny bone (or someone else's).

Joy is contagious…that's why sitcoms have laugh tracks.

O = Open
Promise yourself to be open to new Opportunities—yes, a bonus "O" item, at no extra charge. Not to go all geeky on you, but allow us one more acronym here—there's a cool brain function called **RAS: Reticular Activating System**. Whenever you consciously look for the same thing again and again, it creates a new pathway in your brain that begins to recognize all new instances of whatever it is you're looking for. (It's kind of like push notification on your smart phone.) For example, Oriana collects heart shaped rocks. Not *sorta*-heart-shaped rocks, but unmistakable hearts. Other people walk the same beach for years and never see one. She fills her pockets with them every single day. Same beach. Same rocks. All in plain view. The only difference is that Oriana has a very deep pathway in her brain that alerts her every time she encounters anything heart-shaped. That's RAS in motion. The really cool thing is RAS works for anything: blue Volkswagens, purple pansies, key lime pie, and even abstract concepts like new job opportunities or Mr. Wonderful. We can hear your wheels whirring: *How do I set this up?* Easy peasy…**just program your brain every day by telling yourself what you want it to look for.** (If you want a fancy name for it, it's called neural reconditioning, and a great book on this subject is *The Answer* by John Assaraf and Murray Smith. They go into lots of detail about how it works.) Reprogramming might sound something like this: *In my dream job I have my own office with a big window, in a creative environment where my co-workers smile a lot and seem happy to be there. My work is challenging but fun, and I am well-paid for it. I am open to all avenues which lead me to my perfect new job.* Rinse and repeat throughout the day, and before you know it, you'll start to pick up cues you'd normally miss, leads and tips that may have gone unnoticed. You'll say yes to every lunch offer—you never know

who might point you to a cool opening. You'll read trade magazines you never picked up before and scan Help Wanted sections in the back. Your brain will be working overtime to find you exactly what you state you want. Try it with something simple and work your way up to world peace. **Maintaining an open mind is always a route to greater happiness.**

W = Win
What single achievement would mean today was successful? What would it take to file today in the WIN column? What would make you happy today? You are far more apt to achieve something if you plan for it. Instead of letting another day drift by with no measurable joy or accomplishments, set yourself some metrics to measure it by. It doesn't have to be a big goal. Some days, just getting dressed by noon may be enough. Only you know what a win looks like for you. Then acknowledge and honor your Win. **Even if no one else appreciates what you accomplished, *you* can—and that matters more.**

N = Nudge
We all need motivation from time to time—how would you like to nudge yourself today? What project has been left half done for weeks? How long has it been since you called your mom? What have you been putting off because you're actually afraid to do it? Complacency never got anyone anywhere (except back to the couch). There are few greater joys than doing something you didn't think you could do, or pushing yourself to try something you feared. What are you waiting for? Go nudge yourself!

So there you have it, our simple formula to start your day in big clown shoes:
C: Choose
L: Laugh
O: Open

W: Win
N: Nudge

☺ Remember to schedule happiness…don't just wait and hope it happens! Start each day by seeing it the way you would want it to be.

> **"Nobody really cares if you're miserable,
> so you might as well be happy." ~Cynthia Nelms**

Lunch Launch

Think about it—those of us who go to work five days a week usually take an hour or more for lunch. Unless you're out for a long business meal or having a lunch meeting in your office, then some free time is up for grabs. (If you really spend all 60 minutes eating, then you have more pressing problems!) This is another example of found time. Even if you spend half that time actually eating, **what could you do with the other 30 or more minutes?** Depending on your habits, this can amount to an extra two or three hours per week or eight to twelve hours per month. We bet lots of you spend it reading and answering emails, updating your status on Facebook, texting pals, etc.—all things you may now feel are an essential part of your day. **But hop in the Wayback Machine and recall that just a few years ago we didn't have this technology.** How did you spend your lunchtime then? Today ask:

- Do these techno-time-suckers *really* increase your happiness, or do they just fill your day with busyness?
- How often do you read or share anything of lasting value or importance?
- How many Kardashian reruns can one person really endure?
- What else could you do with those daily 30 minutes to up your happiness level?

Answer: lots! **As long as you know what your true personal values are, then it's easy to make choices that enhance what actually**

matters to you. Perhaps you value a stress-free evening above all else, so for you, running errands at lunchtime makes that possible. Maybe you need to detach from a demanding job, so reading a juicy novel for thirty minutes allows your mind to rest. Yes, Astute Reader, earlier we listed novels as potential distractions—but we also said, it's about making a conscious choice. Maybe decompressing that way each day is a very joyful choice. For someone else, utilizing that extra time to work on a personal goal may make enduring a day job that much easier, as it keeps your own dream alive in your mind.

Don't discount the usefulness of these half hours. If you have a big personal project you're involved in, we challenge you to **keep a running list of Quickie Tasks that can be done in under thirty minutes.** Such as: things that need researching, calls to be made, blog posts that need editing, reading a trade journal, lunching with a mentor, etc. Keep the list with you at all times and relish the joy of accomplishment as you continually cross items off (and add new ones until you're done). You'll be amazed how that can allow you to spend your larger chunks of free time more effectively. So what will you launch on your lunch hour?

"Lost yesterday, somewhere between sunrise and sunset, two golden hours, each set with sixty diamond minutes. No reward is offered, for they are gone forever." ~Horace Mann

Top Ten Reasons We Love Lists
10. Gives clarity to your thoughts
9. Chunks big projects into lotsa smaller ones
8. Nudges your inner slacker to take action
7. Helps organize your messy life
6. Reminds you to buy cat food
5. Holds you accountable for promises
4. Tracks your progress
3. Saves time because you don't have to go back to the store for cat food

2. Prioritizes your time—(move fun higher up your list while you're at it)
And the Number One reason we love lists:
1. Creates excuse for a good gloat once everything is crossed off

Break / Repair

Whenever you take a ***break***, ask yourself what's ***broken*** about your day. Quickly survey your activities and your mood—what's your current **Happy Number**? (See Chapter One.) What immediate shift could you make to zoom it up? Don't let any day drift downward into the dumps—you can turn it around with conscious thought. Let's say you suddenly notice steam curling out of your ears after a co-worker pooh-poohs your hard work. Instead of lashing back with more negativity, what if you simply nod your head and remove yourself to a different physical space where you can regroup? Once out of the bad vibe zone, you can remind yourself of the real truth about your work. You could even ask yourself if there's any merit at all to his criticism. **Every single instance like this when things don't go as you expected is an opportunity to learn, to shift, to revise, to expand.** Can you evaluate your work from a different point of view? Are there any tweaks you could make to enhance it? Or do you just need to leave the building for a few minutes? All of these responses will reduce your stress and keep you from escalating the situation to rat-ass ugly.

Happit: *repairing* For 21 days straight make an appointment at least once a day to check in on your mood. If it needs fixing, do whatever it takes to turn your emotional ship around. No rat-ass ugly days allowed!

Unsentencing your commute

If you have to actually don some apparel and leave the house to go to work, then you're painfully aware of how much joy commuting can drain from your day. Actually it does prove you *can* find pleasure in it. **What would you change about your commute to make it more**

pleasant? Listen to books or podcasts? Learn Mandarin? Dictate a list? Choose music that won't harsh your mellow? Take a slower but quieter route? Ride share and get to know your neighbor? Take your dog to work and let her help plan your day?

Dinner Winner

This is no time to give up on your day. So what if your day went south the minute you arrived at work? So what if your cat hurled hairballs all over your bed? So what if you got stuck in five soul-sucking meetings? So what if you spent an hour gridlocked on the Taconic Parkway? **It's never too late to turn a craptastic day fantastic.** Seriously. What most people do—*and you're not most people, are you?*—is succumb to the flow of the day (or lack thereof). They jump into the River of No Return and ride it with a bottle of red, half a cheesecake and top it off with three hours of nothingness, roaming the 578 channels they work so hard to pay for. But you don't have to do that. You know better—or now you do! **Try thinking of dinner time as a line in the sand**... when you cross it, you leave all the cares of your day behind. You're in new territory now, you're in charge, you control your reaction to your day and you choose your mood. (Sound a little bit familiar?) **Start by thinking of one tiny thing that will shift your attitude.** No, not Jell-O shots. Here are some examples:

- ➡ Call a trusted friend who can be counted on to cheer you up. You're not calling to dump on her, you're calling because talking to her always lightens your mood. She'll probably have you laughing in no time.
- ➡ Watch last night's Letterman or Stewart or Colbert. A DVR is a great investment, because it provides you with humor on demand. It's biologically impossible to feel crappy when you're rolling on the floor laughing.
- ➡ Jot down four things you're grateful for, no matter how small they may seem. Gratitude is a true game changer and mood shifter. It puts your niggling problems in perspective. (Though if you really

did have an Epic Bad Day, then you'll need to take equivalent measures.)
- ➡ Do a good deed. Works every single time. Guaranteed. Helping someone else takes us out of our own self-absorption.
- ➡ Get physical. The fastest way to change your state of mind is to change what you're doing. Walking really does clear your head. Unless of course it's raining cats and dogs, in which case stay inside and crank up some dance music. Or hop on that exercycle that's buried under six layers of clothes. (We have x-ray vision.)
- ➡ Be extra nice to your dog. Get out her best ball. Rub her tummy and enjoy the oxytocin boost. She'll respond with pure glee and that's contagious. Or be extra nice to your cat. Get out the ball he never fetches, and laugh at yourself for ever thinking he would. Give him a treat. Comb the mats out of his fur that you meant to untangle last week. Purr right along.
- ➡ Fix yourself a really nice dinner. Yes, that sounds counter-intuitive. The last thing you may want to do is stand over a hot stove, but nurturing your body with a healthy meal will indeed help you recover, will increase your self-esteem and will set a new precedent for how to treat future episodes of dark-day-itis.

Now you're ready to inject some happiness into the next part of your day.

☺ The more **television** you watch, the less happy you become. People who watch less than two hours of television a day enjoy it more than those who become mesmerized four or more hours. Also, limit the amount of so-called news you watch. It is a non-stop fright parade of negativity. How many more fires / floods / murders / robberies / fatal accidents do you want to pollute your brain and your soul with? Trust us, if anything truly important happens you'll hear about it in other ways. Just want the weather report? Get it online, send it to your phone, and skip the losecast.

Nightly Nudge

There's that word again: nudge. And for good reason. To lead a Big Happy Life you need to be constantly growing, always seeking new ideas and experiences, ever pushing yourself to do what you resist. Okay, not every minute of every day, but pretty darn often. As with your lunch hours, **evenings can represent more found time** that can be put to better use than watching bad singers strive for *their* dreams. Of course, this is often family time, and that's certainly important. Still, we bet there's an extra hour or so to be grabbed for yourself. Maybe not every night, but surely several times a week. If you don't have enough fun in your life, use this time to pursue hobbies. Learn a new craft… perhaps decoupaging the cat who hurled hairballs all over your bed. Start that zombie novel. Take an online class in writing zombie romance novels. Do anything that furthers larger goals you have for yourself, dreams that don't see the light of day during, well, the daytime. How many months or years or decades are you willing to wait to live Your Big Happy Life? *None?* Great! You can start tonight. Free time isn't really free. If you squander it, you've spent it on nothing, which can leave you feeling like you wasted your hard earned money on a fake Rolex. **Consider yourself thoroughly nudged.**

Hot Nudge Sunday

This is a special category of nudginess. Assuming your work week starts on Monday, these are essential ideas to prepare for a happier week ahead. (If you have a different schedule, then adjust accordingly, but then you'll have a Hot Nudge Thursday or whatever, which won't sound as fun, but that's your problem.) This is especially crucial if you have a demanding career or a jam-packed life of any sort that gets extra squirrely as each new week begins. **The idea is to treat yourself to a Sunday evening of preparing for a less stressful Monday.** Take your time to plan Monday in advance: make sure your shirt is ironed, your lunch is made, the kids have their homework ready, there are plenty of diapers in the house, the squirrel DVD is ready to play for the cat—whatever it is that usually goes wrong on Monday, make sure you take care of it on Sunday evening. Create a template list you can use every week for your **Monday Morning Musts**: the things you must do to begin your work week with your head calmly affixed to your neck without whiplash. As part of your Hot Nudge Sunday, do also treat yourself by allowing for some pampering: maybe some yoga, some stretching, a little journaling or meditating—whatever it takes to prepare you for the most important night of sleep, because it sets the tone for your whole (happy!) week. (Sometimes actual fudge might even be called for.) **What makes this Nudge Sunday *Hot* is that this one practice can often prevent a week that cascades out of control like a 30-car pile-up on the interstate.** You, Clever Reader, have much happier weeks to enjoy.

☺Having a bad Monday is a lame way to spend 1/7 of your life.

There you have it. Your entire day detailed with endless opportunities to add more happiness to your life. Some of you (and we know who you are) may be whining just a bit that this all sounds like a lot of *work*...that you'll have to be better *organized*...that you'll have to make *lists*. You know what? You're right. Creating a Big Happy Life does take effort, but haven't we already established that you no longer want a mediocre, middle-of-the-road, mildly boring, mind-numbing life? (If we left out your adjective of choice, feel free to shout it out now. We'll wait.) So get busy and go make a marvelous Monday.

Keep sleep deep
Take it from us on this—cutting back on sleep is NOT the way to make more time for joy. (Unless you've been zeeing away 10 or 12

hours a day.) Both Mike and Oriana have tried the I-can-get-by-with-less-sleep routine. Been there, did that, ruined our health. While the experts can't agree on the magic sleep number, and you aren't wired the same as Peg or Greg, they seem to believe we all should spend between 6-9 hours a night in zonklandia. (Zonk being the key component.) Restless nights of tossing and churning, crammed with nightmares of monstrous looming deadlines do not a happy camper make. So, once you're all tucked in, tell yourself these three things:
1. I have done all I can do today.
2. I deserve a great night's sleep.
3. I enjoy pleasant dreams of My Big Happy Life.

AFFIRMATIONS: I now take charge of my time; this is my life currency and I spend it wisely. I find more and more ways to add happy experiences into my days. I feel a growing inner calm as I organize my life and make more time for what really matters.

In the next chapter…
You can only be happy right now, one moment at a time…so are you happy yet? Tick tock, tick tock. How about now? If not, don't worry. You'll be jumping into joy in the next chapter. How do we know? Because we're going to gently nudge you! The last thing we want to do is push you too hard. But it's still on our list.

Chapter Three
Make Room For More Happiness In Your Life
immersing yourself in joy

In this chapter:
- ✓ Clown College is serious business
- ✓ Jump right into joy
- ✓ Are you having fun yet?
- ✓ Plan to be happy
- ✓ Know what happiness looks like
- ✓ Capture your daily high points
- ✓ Do you know when now is?
- ✓ Surrender to savoring
- ✓ Quintuple your joy
- ✓ Now is always the correct time
- ✓ How far can you bend?
- ✓ Change your thinking
- ✓ Another simple formula: pride = joy
- ✓ Big word, bigger idea
- ✓ Who do you think you are?
- ✓ Whoosh…where did your happiness go?
- ✓ Outdoors, the great
- ✓ Put a pen in your mouth

Getting serious in Clown College

Now we'll pick up Mike's story where we left him in Chapter One…as the happiest farm boy in Indiana, eager to run away and join the circus. His elation at being accepted into the prestigious Ringling Brothers Clown College was his first big payoff for attaining a huge life goal. What that does to your self-esteem is powerful beyond words (but we'll try anyway). The tougher your goal, the richer the reward when you achieve it. For a young guy, especially, it was enormously validating that he had good instincts about his own skills and life path. That he pulled this off with no outside help is really quite astounding. **And that early giant success set Mike up for a lifetime of believing in himself, trusting his gut and going after ever-larger goals.** Of course getting accepted into Clown College was just the first step. Over the next twelve weeks he immersed himself in his exciting new world, but Mike still had to survive the difficult training and then manage to be chosen to perform in the circus.

MIKE EXPLAINS:

"Each day began with an hour of exercise, followed by acrobatics class, trampoline class, a juggling session then off to a wardrobe class, on and on in a long, long day. Most of the aspiring clowns had never done any of those things.

What a surprise—I had to learn how to design and sew my own clown costume! Then on to makeup class where I got to work with the actual circus clowns who taught me how to design and apply the exaggerated makeup. I thought Clown College would be simple and fun…8 hour days…a lovely clown picnic. Ha! It turned out to be non-stop 16-hour days. For most people it was overwhelming. But for me, at 19, I loved it and looked forward to it every single morning. Going to Clown College I learned so many new skills—and I had to learn them quickly—it was total immersion.

It was kind of like *Project Runway* meets the circus. It was like a big reality show with a close-knit group of people, and in the end many of them were indeed sent home. Ringling Brothers was a highly competitive place, because you knew that only half of us were going to make it into the circus. **I always wanted to be the best**, but that was tough to do when there were other people who had a lot more experience than I did. It was important to showcase your talents and shine every day, so when the teachers walked around observing they'd remember you. My goal was to learn as many new skills as I could and wow my teachers. It was important they saw I was a quick learner, because you had to be ready to pick up new routines without a lot of rehearsal. So I'd stay up night and after night just trying to be the best I could be—and I was never happier."

Instead of getting overwhelmed by the many challenges, Mike recognized this as his BIG opportunity to live a **MUCH BIGGER LIFE!** He knew that succeeding at this assignment was his ticket into the circus. Sometimes opportunity starts as a whisper or knocks very quietly on the door of your life. At that point, opportunity shook his door until it burst into smithereens, revealing a huge opening that Mike ran through…right into his Big Happy Life.

Come on, jump right in
Just as Mike had to eat / drink / sleep / live clowning day and night in order to jump into his new life in Clown College, we challenge you to do something similar, to immerse yourself in joy. Don't worry, we aren't suggesting you vault into a vat of lime Jell-O (though come to think of it, that does sound like fun). **Mike wants you to immerse your *mind* and your *heart* in all things joyous for enough time so you really experience happiness in a NEW way.**
Depending on what your starting point is (refer to your Happy Number, Chapter One) you may need to adjust how long you want to spend immersing yourself in good cheer. We urge you to try this for at least a full day, and a weekend would be even better. And while it's meant to be a lot of fun and it may sound easy, we think you'll find it

surprisingly difficult, and therein lies the instructional part. **The degree of difficulty you experience with this exercise reveals how far you may have to travel along the happiness continuum.**

The basic idea is to collect and surround yourself with as many sources of joy as you can, and then spend an entire day or more reveling in those things, smiling and laughing far more than you usually do. You could compare it to foreign language immersion, where you're only allowed to speak Urdu until you learn it. **The specific happy-making sources will be different for each person, but might include:**
- DVDs of your favorite funny films
- A week's worth of DVRed *Daily Show*s, Ellen, Dave, Jimmy or Craig
- Some classic comedy albums—and hey, maybe even a record player if you're going old school
- A collection of *New Yorker* cartoons
- Whatever reading material you find gigglicious (Mike loves his collection of kids jokes from his days as Happy the Hobo)
- Fave family videos—just be sure they're funny—there's no room for the family feud that erupted during Thanksgiving 2007

You may be wondering: Why not just hop on over to that new comedy playing at the gazillo-plex? You'd be better off saving that for another time. There are just too many possibilities for frustration to encroach on your **Really Happy Day** if you try that. You might not find a good parking space, you might be late, the line for Good 'n Plenty might be long 'n windy, the popcorn might be stale, you might sit next to an armrest hog, the movie might stink—you get the picture. *You want guaranteed happiness immersion.*

The goal is to laugh as much as humanly possible in one day. To do this really well may require shutting out the rest of your life for the duration of the experiment. No nagging spouses needed—send them off to the mall or the auto show or the archery range or a spa day. And no whining kidlets allowed either—that's what grandparents are for. You want to be alone with your muses and feel free to laugh out loud uncontrollably without being mocked or teased or otherwise berated. Or perhaps it would be easier for you to simply go away on your own, a mini-getaway to some pleasant spot. However, if it involves sticking your hard working spouse with the kids for the whole weekend, that may be a tough sell. Our advice is to offer him or her the exact same deal for their own **Really Happy Day**. Mike doesn't need to know how you managed it, just make it happen!

Of course there are other components to a Really Happy Day. Food is probably high on your list, so make it extra special too. What foods make you grin in anticipation, make you salivate just thinking about them? Eat those. Even if it means a day of jamoca almond fudge milkshakes with a side of garlic smashed potatoes. Diets be damned—this is not the day to spin a ten-veggie smoothie. (Well there's a chance that could be your happy meal if it really rings your chimes, but if that's true, you probably already have plenty of friends in the vegetable kingdom. Just for today, make some new ones. Go rogue—indulge in ridiculously expensive gourmet cupcakes or a nice vintage red.)

One warning: while it may be tempting to bliss out on booze or other mind altering substances, especially as the day wears on, going too far down that particular rabbit hole will be counterproductive. This is a mental and emotional exercise, so you want to be in control and fully aware of what's going on between your ears—and elsewhere.

Okay, you've made the time and found the place, you've hunted and gathered the grub and you've stockpiled lots of funny stuff. How you actually combine and indulge in it all is *your* design. Just listen to your gut and do whatever feels right at that moment. No one will know if you decide to spend eleven hours in a row yukking it up with the Three Stooges or enjoying a John Cleese/mac-'n-cheese-a-thon. (Can we join you for that one?)

You want to saturate your life in pure joy…**nothing that is not joyful is allowed in your life for that day**. Try and achieve a level of joy-filled intensity you've never felt before. **Really immerse yourself in**

absolute total happiness. One fun idea is to take before and after photos and see how different you look after TJI (Total Joy Immersion).

Okay, then what, you ask. Well, this whole chapter is full of ideas on how you can extend the good vibes, other ways to immerse yourself in joy—though in shorter increments. If you had a great time immersing yourself in happiness, then why not do it again—especially if your life is relatively unencumbered? Also, you might want to journal about your experience. Or blog about it. Or tell your therapist / BFF / Weimaraner about it. **But do think about it.** You might contemplate:

- ☺ What did you learn about yourself?
- ☺ Were you able to indulge yourself without guilt?
- ☺ Did laughter come easily? If not, why not?
- ☺ Could you feel your stress level dissipate?
- ☺ Were you able to access any new or forgotten areas of your mind / self / personality? For example, did you feel like a kid again, or younger in some ways?
- ☺ Did sadness creep in? Did you start to wonder why you didn't do this more often? Did you find it difficult to stay in Your Happy Place emotionally?
- ☺ What activities do you enjoy but rarely find time to do?
- ☺ What did you enjoy the most? Can you figure out how to add more of that sort of thing into your life on a regular basis?

The big point of this experiment is to contrast this new experience of extreme happiness with your regular, perhaps less happy life. Living a **Really Happy Day** is meant as a measuring stick—the bigger the discrepancy, the longer your journey may be to reach Your Big Happy Life. It's also designed to show you viscerally what's possible to attain. Of course, we realize a **Really Happy Day** isn't representative of real life with all its responsibilities, but we hope a taste of it will inspire you to want more—more bliss in your life on a daily basis and more **Really Happy Days** on your calendar.

"Time you enjoy wasting, was not wasted." ~John Lennon

☺ **Are you having fun yet?**
Mike dares you to do this at random moments during your day—especially when a whiff of frustration wafts by. Pop Quiz…**Ask yourself: Am I doing this activity because I enjoy it and value it?** The more often you can answer "yes," the happier you'll be. Here's a reality check: for every minute you're angry, you lose sixty seconds of happiness. So why would you choose to dwell in anger? Or even just plain old grumpiness? Weather got you down? Get over it. Tell yourself what a glorious day it is, no matter where you are or what the weather is doing. Try to simply enjoy the fact that you're alive. It sure beats the alternative.

"When you rise in the morning, think of what a precious privilege it is to be alive; to breathe, think, to enjoy, to love." ~Marcus Aurelius

"The primary cause of unhappiness is never the situation but your thoughts about it." ~Eckhart Tolle

Make every day special—even in a small way
Now let's generate some smiles in your real life. Think back over the last several weeks…how many special episodes of real joy can you recall? How about the last few days…how much genuine happiness can you remember feeling? You aren't alone if you can't name much of anything. The sad truth is that for most of us, the majority of our days pass by devoid of much to celebrate or even recall just a few days later. Our days pile up around us like so many leaves at the base of an oak tree, their life drained and faded. We shuffle through them unaware of the wasted opportunities, of the repetitive boredom and our own numbness.

We're overworked, over-scheduled, and even though we use wireless devices, we're still way too tied to them. We may have done away with the electrical cords, but we might as well be physically tethered to our jobs, our families and all our various responsibilities.

How often do you really unplug and disconnect completely? Rarely if ever, Mike suspects.

It doesn't have to be like that. What if instead, you could experience your life as a scrapbook of days, with each page displaying mementos of really happy moments and experiences? What if every day you collected those images in words, snapshots, videos, ticket stubs, notes, or yes—even bright oak leaves pressed between the pages of your book? (More on preserving your joy later.) But first you need to create those moments, and we believe the more *intention* you focus on that plan, the more it will happen. **Happy really does happen when you plan for it.**

For example, let's say you're just about to go to the same old sandwich shop for lunch, when you decide to do something better and have a happy meal instead. Not that kind. A *real* happy meal. Perhaps the night before you anticipated this and prepared a sack lunch. Or you might whip through a drive-through or grab any kind of take-out food. It's not about the food—it's about where you're going to eat it—which is anywhere out of the ordinary. If you're so inclined and have time to go to a park or some other beautiful outdoor space, then that could be a great pick. Watch for swans or hummingbirds or daffodils poking their slender shoots out of the ground. Soak up some rays. Take off your shoes.

But this is your happy meal. Perhaps you'd prefer strolling along a new street in a different neighborhood until you find a bench, then settling in for some people watching. (Remember to smile!) Or maybe you're off to a museum or a brown bag concert in the plaza. Maybe you keep a football in your trunk or even a skateboard and make time to play a bit. We know someone who loves to drop in at a doggy daycare center just to watch the ever-changing horde of pooches and puppies playing with wild abandon. That's sure to make you laugh. **The point is to leap out of your rut.** Shake up your life. Who knows what might happen when you put yourself in new settings. All kinds of great ideas might wander into your mind. All sorts of interesting people might cross your path. If you do this often enough (and pay attention while you're at it), we promise you some wonderful things will happen. Things worthy of remembering, worthy of placing in your scrapbook of days.

Snap some photos of the strange clouds passing by, or take a video of gulls hitching a ride on a passing tugboat. Though just because you have your phone in your pocket, doesn't mean you HAVE to check it obsessively or spend your precious lunch hour texting and reading emails. Mike's advice is to *escape* your ruts, not just move them to another locale. **The idea is to be here now (and only here)—wherever here is.** Heck, you could even meditate or read something inspirational. You might jot down some haiku or indulge any sort of creative expression. You might review some happiness affirmations or just think loving thoughts about someone dear to you.

Like any other newly acquired habit, making quality time for yourself every day can be learned and ingrained until it becomes an automatic desire. Besides, a genuine break in your day can go miles toward reducing your stress level, which leads to greater productivity, a happier you at work, better health, and on and on in a daisy chain of happy events. Because you're more productive in the afternoon, you take less work home in the evening, which gives you more time to spend with your family, which makes everyone feel better, and on and on. *All because you leapt out of your ruts.* Life isn't measured by the breaths we take but the moments that take our breath away.

"The habit of turning a trail into a rut must be incessantly fought against if one is to remain alive." ~Edith Wharton

**"Be happy for this moment. This moment is your life!"
~Omar Khayyam**

MIKE CONTINUES HIS STORY:

"I always learned something from everything I witnessed in Clown College, and I made a point of writing down my takeaways in a notebook. I was teased for it, because no one else was taking notes, but I knew there was a lot of wisdom being passed down, and I didn't want to forget any of it. Even though it was Clown College, I took it very seriously. Life is about awareness and observations, and I wanted to capture all my good times and everything I was learning so I could study it later. Looking back now, I see that training to balance strange objects was a good metaphor for learning to create balance in various areas of my life. My takeaway from juggling class was that you can do so much more than you think you can do if you're taught in the right way."

Know what happiness looks like

If you can't identify what makes you happy, you'll never get to truly enjoy it. We know you're thinking about it, because you're reading this book. Happiness is so much more than celebrating the obvious milestones in our lives. Start small by thinking about the simple delights that may have tinted your day a nicer shade of sunny yellow.

- What pleased you when you looked out a window?
- What did your child or dog or cat do to tickle your fancy?
- What aromas helped you recall a pleasant memory?
- Who surprised you with a call or email?
- What snippet of music lifted your mood?
- Who gave you a compliment or some kind words of encouragement today?

It's so easy to rush right by the daily opportunities most of us have to experience happiness. We often discount those brief glimpses and moments of joy, because they seem less important or because they aren't Big Events. However, we contend that **those numerous tiny moments of grace that occur throughout our days are the true essence of living a happy life**. Letting them whiz by unappreciated can make your life feel less joy filled.

Here's a truth you may need more years on your bones to appreciate, but trust us: absolutely enjoy the sweet moments, the little things that color your days, because one day you may well look back at your life and realize those were the big things…that *is* leading a Big Happy Life.

Happit: *capturing* One solution is to learn to consciously notice these simple daily delights and slow down long enough to really experience them. To say *Yes, this makes me happy. This is why I (fill in the blank) every day. This makes life worth living.* You do this by developing self-awareness, by easing up your pace and becoming alert to joy in all its forms. Then once you train yourself to spot and relish these flashes of happiness, **the next step is to capture them**. If you don't think of yourself as creative, then besides being a lie because we're ALL creative, this part may sound like too big a project. But in fact, it's an essential part of living a Big Happy Life.

Capturing your happy moments may be as simple as jotting down a few sentences each night that help you remember the high points of your day. Or it may be as elaborate as creating a full-on multi-media scrapbook of your life. There is no way to emphasize enough how much value these efforts will have in later years as you—and your loved ones if you so choose—review these joyful times and relive them all over again. It can be enormously instructive to your family members to see what you've valued in your life, what has enriched your time here. These records of your life can become permanent keepsakes that document the Technicolor texture of your Big Happy Life. However you decide to capture your happy moments, be sure to do so for 21 days in a row. Happiness is not measured by the number of days you live but, rather, by the number of days you remember.

"Plenty of people miss their share of happiness, not because they never found it, but because they didn't stop to enjoy it." ~William Faulkner

The foolish man seeks happiness in the distance; the wise man grows it beneath his feet. ~Openheim

"The key to joy is to be easily pleased. Light is in the broken bottle as well as in the diamond." ~Mark Nepo

"It is of the small joys and little pleasures that the greatest of our days are built." ~Mary Anne Radmacher

Do you know when now is?
Yes, that sounds like a silly question. But many people spend so much of their time either rehashing the past or fantasizing about the future that they miss many of their *now* moments. To be clear—some fond recollecting of happy times gone by is a good thing, as is constructive visioning of a better future for yourself. What's pointless and debilitating is endless reliving of old negativity, replaying old arguments and hurts in an endless loop of blame and shame. And just as damaging is remaining stuck in dreams of your future without ever taking any *action* to bring them to life. Both those activities suck the *now* out of your soul, and those minutes and hours can never be reclaimed. You've squandered them forever—but we're here to help you stop doing that.

So what helps you live in the now? What activities so enthrall you that you can think of nothing else while you're doing them? Notice experiences that make you *feel* your life as you're living it. Maybe it's kayaking on a cool morning, or walking in a pine forest at dawn or teaching your daughter her ABCs. Very likely most, if not all, of your senses are engaged. **Think about which senses impact you the most.** Are you more auditory—do you respond most to music, spoken words and your son's laughter? Or are you more visual—do you remember events as pictures and movies in your mind? **Once you identify your most responsive senses, you can design your life to include more expressions of those.**

For example, if you realize how important your soundscape is and how much you dread the cacophony in your office, then you can do whatever it takes to bring music or perhaps nature sounds into your work space to drown out your co-workers' discussions of basketball, football or slacker husbands.

The more senses you engage at a time, the richer the experience you'll have. **Savoring with all your senses helps reveal the deep beauty and meaning in everything.** The French have *Joie d'vive*, Italians have *la dolce vita*, but most Americans only have a Happy Hour, which is often just an excuse for a gripe session. Why limit happy to just an hour? (Even if margaritas are included.) We need a pervasive sense of how to infuse *all* aspects of life with deeper levels of happiness. It's in the details, for example:

★ Look for ways to **add visual stimulation** to the places where you spend the most time: inside your car; on your desk; in your kitchen—wherever it is—add more color and inspiring imagery to lift your mood.

★ The same applies to touch: **add more textures** you find appealing and comforting—high thread count sheets, a cashmere shawl, a thick rug, leather wrapped steering wheel, cushiony insoles, ergonomically fabulous kitchen implements with great rubber grips.

★ **Control your aural environment:** stop and really listen in all the places where you spend significant time. What do you hear? Have you tuned out annoying traffic, your neighbor's noisy Norwich Terrier, your kids' endless bickering? Time to really drown it all out—add personal soundscapes that support your intentions in each space and time. Enjoy music or sounds of nature to fit your endeavor, whether it's relaxation, exercise or creative thinking. Don't suffer in the strangle of negative noise.

★ Apply that thinking to your sense of smell and **design your olfactory environment**. Experiment with aromatherapy, essential oils, colognes, perfumes, candles, etc. There's even a room spray that smells like fresh baked bread! Make your own potpourri blends. Fashion your own personal fragrance with the help of a perfumier. Learn which flowers you respond to the most deeply, and surround yourself with them. Banish and avoid smells you don't like: cigarette smoke, mildew, cabbage cooking, a ripe litter box.

★ The last sense needs the least explanation, as most of us already take a lot of control over what we taste. But perhaps if we don't prepare our own food, we don't indulge as many of our preferences are we could. Learn to cook some of your favorite dishes, and **learn to savor** what you eat by taking more time with your meals. Tickle your taste buds by being adventurous and finding new foods to add to your list of ones that delight you. Grow your own herbs, try exotic spices—besides they aren't just embellishments, they're really good for you too. Don't fall into ruts of eating the same six meals over and over.

☺Yesterday is history. Tomorrow is a mystery. Today is a gift. That's why we call it the present.

**"Be happy in the moment, that's enough.
Each moment is all we need, not more."** ~Mother Teresa

**"We stopped at perfect days and got out of the car."
~R. Brautigan**

**"It is possible to live happily in the here and now.
So many conditions of happiness are available—more than enough for you to be happy right now. You don't have to run into the future in order to get more."** ~ Thich Nhat Hanh

Surrender to savoring

So what is that, exactly? ***Savoring*** *is the ability to prolong and extend enjoyment, a willingness to pause and notice details and your emotional reactions.* It's a way of stretching those NOW moments. It's the difference between dashing to your car because it's started to rain and stopping for a deep breath of green-scented air then realizing the grass is growing again, that spring is edging into your life. It's the difference between wolfing down your fettuccine Alfredo and lingering over each creamy bite. In fact, studies prove a direct correlation between the amount of time someone spends eating a piece of chocolate and the satisfaction they derive from it.

But wait, there's more! For those of you who enjoy concepts quantified, here are the **Official Four Stages of Savoring** as determined by guys who get paid big bucks to study such things:

1. Anticipate the thing you're going to savor—which doesn't work so well with watching a hummingbird or your Maine coon cat chasing a leaf. With other things, it's a great way to prepare yourself for the real deal. (We talked about this more in Chapter One, in fact it is our first Happit.)

2. Appreciate the event. Stay in the present and feel every last moment of it…allow it to be vivid, bright, lush or ever so subtle. Listen to the mallards skimming the lake as they touch down, then a flutter of wings as they shake off water.

3. Remember the feelings. Reminiscing with fellow travelers or partygoers deepens the experience, as does reviewing photos or videos of the event. (Just don't become so caught up in recording your special times that you don't really savor them.) Bring back mementos to keep the experience alive; a tiny shell on your desk can recapture an entire week in the Caymans.

4. Share the experience with others—before, during and after. Looking forward to a party with friends, talking about a magnificent sunset with your honey, discussing a concert on Twitter afterwards, all sustain the experience, give the good times more space in your mind. Finding kindred spirits who share your passions enriches the enjoyment of them.

"A positive mind anticipates happiness, joy, health and a successful outcome of every situation and action." ~Remez Sasson

"Much happiness is overlooked because it doesn't cost anything."
~Unknown

While you can revisit something you savored in the past and anticipate something you hope to savor later in the day, **genuine, industrial strength savoring can only be done in this very moment.** Now. Here. So if you'd like to experience more *nows* in your day, learn to savor more. The more you can prolong positive experiences, the more positive sensations are filling up your day, which—guess what—equals happiness.

Here's a secret: when you master savoring, you can experience natural highs that supersede anything that comes from a bottle (unless perhaps what you're savoring is a fine vintage). This is the sort of bliss that poets call a true union with nature, observing an eagle so intently that when it soars skyward you feel the pull of the wings in your own shoulders.

Mike reminds us not to settle for the ordinary and mundane—keep reaching for the extraordinary, and learn to savor *all* of life more fully. **Happiness is something which is constantly happening**, like the wind—you just have to let yourself feel it. If you live only for the future, you will not be present when it arrives. Instead, we urge you to **seek the deeper experience of joy that is available in daily life**, experiences that don't depend on whether A B or C happens. Savor the present moment and feel the kind of happiness which is untouched by time. The future starts today, not tomorrow. Nothing that happened yesterday can limit the possibilities today.

☺**POP QUIZ:** Find happiness through savoring...how many positive events have occurred in the last hour? If you really look for them, you may be surprised. If you're telling yourself: *I'll be happy when____* you're caught in the illusion. Have you noticed the goal posts are always moving?

**"The whole of reality is contained in the present moment.
If you have your full attention in the moment, you will see only joy."
~Deepak Chopra**

**"Ever since happiness heard your name, it has been running
through the streets trying to find you." ~Hafiz-e Shirazi**

☺**Now is always the correct time.** When trying to live more in the now, avoid the pitfall of dithering, of wavering between options. Remaining too long in an indecisive space puts your life on hold. Precious moments when you could be savoring life are simply tossed aside. If this is your issue, start with smaller things of little consequence and force yourself to choose quickly. No more vacillating over menus or which shoes to buy. Pick something! (And be glad you don't wear size 28!) Then escalate the game to ever more important decisions. When you're sure, take action, don't wait, do it NOW! The rush you'll feel is momentum as you break free from the bonds of indecision. Don't wait for the perfect moment—take the moment and make it perfect! *Whee!*

How far can you bend?

A classic hallmark of a happy person is the ability to be flexible, to adapt to change easily, quickly and with good humor. Mike's time in Clown College certainly taught him that. One of the best things about it was that he got to train with some of the greatest teachers in the world. Many of them were fourth and fifth generation circus performers, world-class entertainers from thirteen different countries. Most of them were multi-talented, able to do all sorts of acts, whether it was tumbling or balancing or a horse act. His juggling teacher could juggle seven clubs really well, which was amazing. *You* throw seven oranges in the air and see what happens—we guarantee you'll get some juice!

There have only been four Master Clowns, and Mike got to study with the three remaining ones. (Emmett Kelly had already died by the time Mike got to Ringling.) The three he studied with were: Bobby Kaye, Frosty Little and Lou Jacobs. Lou was the most famous—he was 6'4" with a little hat on his pointy head, and he had a Chihuahua called Knucklehead. He was best known for driving into the circus ring with his dog in a tiny car about two-feet tall. Then this huge guy would unfold himself and emerge from the car, which was always astounding to watch. Lou was a supreme contortionist, and he's the only clown ever honored with being on a postage stamp.

MORE MIKE:
"A big surprise in Clown College was that I had to sing and dance. Since I'd never even *seen* the circus, I had no clue. I had to be in three big numbers singing and dancing. While I don't have much of a singing voice, I made up for it with enthusiasm. But the biggest surprise was how many different things we had to learn. I thought Clown College was going to be easy. If someone arrived as a magician, they didn't realize they were also going to have to learn to juggle and so on."

Are you the sort of person who loves to stir the pot of your life, or do you run screaming from major changes, resisting all the way? Resistance breaks flow, slows energy and is almost always futile, since some kind of change is inevitable. While your attitude toward change may be partly innate temperament, like most things, you can transform how you think about it if you choose to. How would you react if you were suddenly told you had to sing and dance on stage? Mike adapted by improving his dance skills—which was something he *could* do—and singing very softly so he couldn't really be heard.

Change your thinking
One key to adaptive behavior is to first change how you think about happiness. Instead of spending so much of your time thinking about all the things you *don't* have that would make you happy, **spend your time thinking about the things you *do* have already that make**

you happy. The happiest people don't necessarily have the best of everything, they just make the most of everything they have, never taking anything for granted.

Mike admits he's lucky he was born with a joyful spirit, but he still worked to cultivate his all-out positive attitude. He just doesn't make room in his mind or spirit for negative ideas. Even when faced with daunting challenges, he finds a way to turn each one into a learning experience. He believes he's in charge of his own destiny—and that negativity isn't part of it. He simply changes one thought at a time.

Another way to look at it is to think in ***victor* language, not *victim* language**. No matter how bad you think your life is, we guarantee you there are other people who are worse off than you are. Find something positive to hang onto, no matter how small. When Mike discovered he had to create his own clown costume and pay for everything himself, he couldn't afford a high-quality professional wig like most of the students were able to buy. Instead of a yak wig (yesiree, they wear yak fur on their heads!), Mike made do with a cheap acrylic fiber wig, which didn't hold up well at all in the rigorous circus schedule. Instead of letting it get him down or allow it to affect his performance, he just accepted the teasing and learning to give as good as he got. After all, he was over-the-moon happy to be in the circus, yak or no yak on his head.

It may help to take an **inventory of any chronic negative thoughts** that interfere with your positive outlook. Look at which excuses you go to first to blame a bad attitude on:
- not enough time
- not enough money
- not enough help
- not enough training
- not enough clarity

Behind all of those is a mind shift waiting to happen:
- I can make time, I can watch less TV, be more productive
- I can spend less money, save more money, borrow or earn more
- I can ask for more help, become more efficient

- I can ask for training, study online, read books, find a mentor
- I can ask for more clarity on my assignment, get it in writing

Separate fact from fiction! **What's really true about your circumstance, and what can you do to change it for the better?** It's your life—choose to change it however you darn please! If you can't change it, change the way you think about it. Pick good thoughts. Choose a happy outlook. Nobody likes a sourpuss. (Do try this at home.)

Happit: *shifting* Practice shifting your thinking at least once a day for 21 days, from a negative assumption or point of view to a more positive one.

> "We either make ourselves miserable, or we make ourselves happy. The amount of work is the same." ~Carlos Castaneda

> "Some people feel the rain. Others just get wet." ~Bob Marley

> "I discovered I always have choices, and sometimes it's only a choice of attitude." ~Judith M. Knowlton

One secret of happiness is found in your daily routine. You'll never change your life until you can improve recurring aspects of your day. **Think about the most unpleasant part of your typical day.** What is it? Getting up so damn early? Walking Scruffy before dawn? Rush hour traffic? Interminable meetings? Too tired to fix a healthy dinner? Identify your Number One Daily Awful, then focus on transforming that, because fixing the worst part of your day will yield the most bang for your self-help buck. **Don't just slide into grumbling acceptance of a negative experience—there's always something proactive you can do.** Change your schedule, shift your sleep patterns, hire a dog walker, go in earlier to beat the rush, reinvent your staff meetings to be more productive—and gasp!—even more fun, cook for the week on Saturday, and so on. **Don't accept negatives in your life that you can do something about**—and you *can* do something about most of them!

Scientists who study happiness claim that 40 percent of our happiness is created by our daily thoughts and acts. So what will you do to make the happiest use of your 40 percent today?

"If you do what you've always done, you'll get what you've always gotten." ~Ed Foreman

"Don't wait until conditions are perfect to begin. Beginning makes conditions perfect." ~Alan Cohen

☺ We're constantly surprised by what a big happiness boosts we get from small changes. As Samuel Johnson wrote, "It is by studying little things that we attain the great art of having as little misery, and as much happiness as possible."

Another simple formula: pride = joy

Back in Clown College Mike dealt with the barrage of new skills to learn by simply working harder and longer than his competitors. (Remember, half of them were going to be sent home.) Intense hard work has always been a component of manifesting most goals worth achieving, but sometimes that gets forgotten in our age of instant gratification.

Just watch those shows on HGTV that feature first-time home buyers who won't settle for anything less than their dream home with the trendiest high-end finishes. Whatever happened to fixer-uppers, to taking pride in transforming your first home from a beast to a beauty? Surely you can recall something you did that took a lot of effort and how good you felt on the other end of it? That's always a route to joy.
Rediscover self-reliance for a good jolt of joy.

MIKE'S STILL TALKING:
"I found myself staying up later and later practicing, trying to master each new skill. Sometimes my life was out of control chaos. I had to learn to make do with less and less sleep. My muscles were in pain, my mind was overloaded. When I called home my parents would ask how I was doing, and I'd say: *Well today I can barely walk, but I'm LOVING it!* Some people found the pressures exhausting, but for me, being away from home for the first time and actually living the very dream I'd been focused on for three years was exhilarating. My happiness level was sky-high."

For Mike, everything was new and exciting, as if his small town life had been lived in black and white, and he was suddenly thrust into a full-blown Technicolor world of delights. What helped him succeed was his great attitude. He chose to grow and change and adapt to whatever was thrown his way, so he was, indeed, noticed for his dedication. At the end of Clown College they performed a three-hour show as their final audition, and **Mike was chosen as one of the 29 new clowns from the 4,600 who applied that year.** And boy-oh-boy was he rightfully proud!

Big word, bigger idea
In fact, there's a fancy name for that: **eudaimonia**, which is a *higher* form of happiness, and means striving toward excellence based on your unique talents and potential. It's a more enduring type of happiness than the fleeting pleasures of food, drink and so on. Those busy happiness researchers believe that eudaimonic well-being is more important. Aristotle considered it to be the noblest goal in life. In our era we'd call it personal growth, or aiming to fulfill the promise of your Highest Self. Eudaimonia also embodies continually taking on new challenges and fulfilling what you believe to be your purpose in life.

"Eudaimonic well-being is much more robust and satisfying than hedonic happiness, and it engages different parts of the brain," says researcher Richard J. Davidson, PhD." **Eudaimonia is also good for the**

body. Women who scored high on psychological tests for it because they were purposefully engaged in life and pursued personal development, also weighed less, slept better and had fewer stress hormones and markers for heart disease than other study participants. And that includes those who reported plenty of the hedonic type of happiness, according to a study led by Carol Ryff, PhD, a professor of psychology at the University of Wisconsin.

> **"Experiment with your life. That is what you have it for."**
> **~Gary Zukav**

Who do you think you are?
   The single most important task for a new clown is to figure out his circus persona. What personality did he want to portray? What gender, what age, what tone? It was a highly creative assignment, one that Mike rose to with glee.

MIKE HAS MORE TO SAY:
   "I had to figure out who I would be in the circus, an alter ego. I had to decide what sort of shoes I'd wear, what kind of wig and so on. I had to create my whole costume and makeup…what would my nose look like? By the time I got there I had zero money and didn't know I'd be expected to buy parts of my costumes. Because I couldn't afford an expensive yak hair wig, all the other clowns teased me. After my first tumbling act, the hair in my wig started to fall out, so **here's a great life tip: always go with the yak hair wig!**
   I learned the importance of how things were made and fastened together. I'd never sewed a day in my life and my costume looked terrible, but luckily there were people there to help us. Custom clown shoes are also really expensive and have to be durable to withstand so many shows. Some of the costumes I wore in the big production numbers (which Ringling did supply) cost $7,000. each, and we had to wear them and preserve them for a couple of years. To design my own

clown persona I studied hundreds of the famous clowns and chose from them the various aspects of my look. Some days we had to be in makeup for 16 hours, constantly fixing it and resetting every few hours. Chaos was the norm. That's the great thing about life…life should be about change, about trying things in different ways, about being brave, being a little wild and edgy. You have to adapt, change and be willing to try anything in order to live this great big magical life."

While some of Mike's fellow new clowns chose to adopt a sad personality, Mike tellingly decided he wanted to project a happy, fun-loving character. Developing his clown persona taught Mike the importance of self-knowledge. Here's the cool thing: even though you're not designing a clown persona, **you ARE designing your own self-image all the time.** Who do you think you are? Who do you want to be? What do you choose to wear? Mostly black or gray? Bright prints? Pale neutral colors that allow you to fade into the background? What do those choices say about you? How's your grooming? What sort of style do you project? Are you the urban hipster who always knows the best place to get sushi? **Congruity between what you want to project and the reality of your life = a path to more happiness.**

Happit: *cheer up* **Consciously demonstrate a different aspect of yourself in a more cheerful manner every day for 21 days straight.** Wear brighter colors, a flower in your lapel, a silly button, a Daffy Duck watch, a wacky hat, or even just a colorful pocket handkerchief if you work in one of those repressed offices. Or one day you might bring a vase of dahlias to work, or a homemade lemon meringue pie, or recycle a box of books and magazines with your co-workers. Perhaps you make a fuss over your neighbor's birthday or organize a book group lunch at a nicer-than-usual bistro. It matters not what you do, just that you demonstrate a happier state of being in some way every day, no two days the same. What will amaze you (and that's a promise) is the effect this will have not just on you, but on everyone you come into contact with.

Like a pebble tossed into water, your cheerfulness will radiate outward and affect all the inhabitants of your metaphorical pond.

☺ **Take a cue from nature, the great transformer:** from chrysalis to butterfly, tadpole to frog, bud to bloom—how would you like to transform yourself? Inventing and manifesting a new version of yourself can bring enormous amounts of happiness into your life. Just ask anyone who has shed 100 pounds or more, or someone who has worked their way to a PhD or someone who has gone from homeless to homeowner. What BIG joyful project could you immerse yourself in?

> "Always be yourself. Unless you can be a unicorn.
> Then be a unicorn." ~Some Sillyperson

Replace your same-old, same-old

With some brand-new, brand-new. Think about any boring routines you've succumbed to…are there any you're ready to shatter? Complacency can be so seductive because it's easy, that well-trod Path of Least Resistance. At the next fork in your road, try a different route, the road less explored. That was the easy part for Mike. There's nothing like hitting the road with the Greatest Show on Earth to yank you out of any routines. No two days were ever alike, and only the flexible survived and thrived. Luckily, Mike was ideally suited to life on a circus train.

Think about the journey: As you map out what you want in life and how you're going to get it, **focus on the experiences** you have getting there. It really is the journey toward your goals that becomes the meat of your experience and creates the most happiness. For Mike, he found as much joy in his literal journey riding and living on the circus train as he did performing in the circus. It was full-on 24/7 joy immersion!

> **"Happiness is not a state to arrive at but a manner of traveling."**
> **~Margaret Runbeck**

MORE STUFF MIKE SAID:

"Amazingly, my childhood fantasies of becoming a clown matched up fairly well with my actual experience, but the reality was even more exciting than I could have envisioned. We all lived on a circus train, which was over a mile long and carried 200 people from over 30 different countries. (Thus the need to know up front if we were claustrophobic.) There was always something wild and wonderful happening on the train, and I got to hang out with and get to know all kinds of people—even when they didn't speak English. It was such a fun experience for a young guy from a small Indiana farm town.

I had to learn how to really get along with people, what motivated them, what they wanted or didn't want, how to become part of the group. In school I was kind of a loner, not on teams, preferring to learn one-on-one skills. So in the circus I had to learn cooperation. Never having seen a circus, I didn't know what I was getting into. All I knew was I wanted to be funny and make people laugh. **I wanted to have the most fun possible at the time and live a joyful and happy existence.**

With Ringling Brothers you end up trying out for different specialties, and I became part of the comedy trapeze team. It's a good thing I was really young, because I had to spin around then fall and hit the ground with perfect timing. I had to develop comedic sensitivities of my own and learn how to react to and play off other people. In other words, how to be funny as a group—which was entirely different from mouthing off for laughs in geometry class."

> **"There is no way to happiness. Happiness is the way."**
> **~ Thich Nhat Hanh**

People either loved it or hated being in the circus. Some people missed their families or they didn't think it paid well enough, or they didn't like being around strangers. But Mike loved it, and money wasn't a factor at all. He savored arriving in each new city and exploring it.

MIKE REMEMBERS:

"If you were adventurous and were adaptable to change, then that was one of the magical things about circus life. I'd find all sorts of bookstores in each town and grab new books to immerse myself in. I loved learning new things and was always looking for new ways to inspire and motivate myself."

☺ **Personal growth and helping others are more likely to promote happiness than pursuing money and status.** Studies show that experiences are valued more than accumulating stuff. Scientists found that American millionaires living in mansions are barely happier than Masai warriors in Kenya who live in huts. Mike had no permanent home while in the circus and not a lot of money, but he enjoyed some of the richest days of his life living on that crowded, noisy circus train. Spend money to do things, to go places, to have experiences—as opposed to accumulating more stuff. **Experiences last a lifetime. The crap you bought at Costco won't.**

Happit: *belonging* Find some kind of group to join. We're social animals, and even the loners among us need some socializing. Belonging to a group—even if it only gathers once a month—delivers the same amount of happiness as doubling your income! Plus it's a great way to find allies, mentors and mastermind partners. If the purpose of the group is altruistic, you can get an even bigger boost by helping other people. **There is only ONE thing the happiest people all over the world have in common: they enjoy broad and deep personal support networks.** One of the best ways to enlarge yours is to join some groups of like-minded people. Then try this challenge: **Every day for the first 21 days after you find a group you like, do at least one thing to stay engaged**

with the group. Call someone in the group, email a leader with thanks, have lunch with a new pal, volunteer to be on a committee, attend every function, offer to bring some healthy snacks, and so on.

"Shared joy is a double joy; shared sorrow is half a sorrow."
~Swedish proverb

Finding joy in online socializing

As long as you maintain a balance between virtual friends and ones you can give an actual hug, participating in social media can do a lot to enhance your happiness level and even help you savor key moments. We want to encourage a community of joy-seeking people to share their happy moments and discoveries, so we've created a space for you at our website. We suggest that at some point you share your own vision and progress with the public. (Anonymously if you prefer.) By making your dreams public you open up to feedback, support and yes, nudging. You might post part or all of your vision for Your Big Happy Life on Facebook; you might tweet or blog about your progress or engage whatever social media interwebiness you prefer.

We've even provided daily prompts to inspire your conversations. Feel free to adapt these and integrate them into your happy practices:

One Ray Monday: Share ONE small bit of sunshine…a quote, a link, a happy ending…then tap into the collective happy pond throughout the day to see what others have posted whenever you need a lift.

Tickle Me Tuesday: Chip in some chuckles and contribute things that make you smile or laugh.

Wake Me Up Wednesday: Send out jolts of energizing ideas, images, videos—whatever gets you through Hump Day. Cheer up, cheer in, cheer out, cheer all around.

Yourday Thursday: Contribute ideas to pamper yourself, focus on your own projects, boost your confidence, and so on.

Tryday Friday: Declare what new things you're trying, or make a dare, suggest a way to stretch yourself or have an adventure.

Don't Sit Saturday: Super important if you sat all week, share what you're going to do to get going. Every new day is another chance to change your life.

Funday Sunday: Discuss novel ways to inject more fun in your life and document what you did with photos, videos or perhaps some iambic pentameter.

☺ "I can't tweet at the moment, I'm simulating happiness on Facebook," is undoubtedly all true for some people. While social media can be an entertaining playground, to reap true happiness from it, just be sure the joy you share is genuine! Painting a fictional picture of your life online is a recipe for an attitude crash, once reality rears its dismal head. Instead, focus on doing something to improve your life so you DO have something fabulous to report to your 782 friends. (Keep reading this book, for example!)

> **"Happiness is defining yourself by what you ARE, not by what you're NOT." ~Dr. Happy**

Happit: *listening* Monitor your thoughts and words. Listen to yourself—how often do you use negative words, how often do you criticize, gossip or otherwise spread bad vibes? Mom was right: If you can't say something good about someone, shut your pie hole. How hard are you on yourself? Do you dismiss your own ideas before they even poke their heads out of the ground? Ridding your vocabulary of downer words and phrases can allow a lot more sunshine in your soul. For 21 days straight (no cheating) keep a written record of at least one incident a day when you correct yourself and flip your words in a better direction.

The power of the split second

Has this ever happened to you: You're humming along having a perfectly decent day, when out of the blue you start to feel sad or angry, perhaps even tear up a bit—all for no apparent reason? Then before you know it, other negative emotions start to edge into your mind, you find yourself easily distracted, feeling more tired than usual and so on, until your fine day has taken a turn for the plug ugly. Yet later, when you try and figure out why, you're unable to pinpoint the cause, so you chalk it up to a poor night's sleep or low blood sugar or that moody email from your boss.

Here's the secret: it's nearly impossible to deconstruct what went wrong once a few minutes have elapsed. Why? Because what caused your sudden shift in mood were likely *micro-thoughts* and feelings—some so fleeting they didn't even register in your conscious mind. And yet they absolutely impacted how you felt and how your day dissolved into low productivity pond sludge and added stress.

And here's the solution: Learn to monitor your thoughts and feelings and be especially vigilant for those *micro-events*. These can be twinges of emotional pain or brief pangs of longing or fleeting feelings of exhaustion that lead directly to thoughts that begin to undermine your day. Thoughts of wanting another cup of coffee or a donut or a shopping excursion at lunchtime or just wandering aimlessly around YouTube vaguely in search of something uplifting. These twinges last less than a second, so if you don't notice them immediately, they just become background unhappiness which can build and build until you're really having a craptastic day.

Here's a real example from Oriana's life to show you how it works. "One ordinary January day I was working at my desk when I thought about a particular client who I knew was off on vacation in Hawaii. My first thought was how happy I was knowing that all my work for him was up to date. My second thought was how nice it was to have a whole week without any emergency projects from him. So far so good. But then a millisecond later I caught a whiff of sadness and felt myself start to tear up. What was that about? When I examined the gap in my thinking, I realized that a **third micro-thought** had whizzed right past my conscious mind: *I was envious of my client off in sunny, warm Hawaii, while I was stuck here working in chilly, damp Washington state.* In addition to that, I also resented my client's vacation, because I had failed to take enough time off myself last year, and so was feeling an extra high level of exhaustion.

Those micro-thoughts triggered my sadness, and that tiny glimpse of my overly tired self caused me to cry. This entire episode transpired in about two seconds, and if I hadn't been paying attention, it would have festered beneath my surface until I chose some probably unhealthy way of expressing it.

Once I examined those thoughts and feelings, I could add to the list some anger at myself for not taking better care of my health—didn't I deserve nice vacations too? Why was I working so darn hard anyway? How come I never seem to find time to go somewhere warm and comforting in the winter? With very little effort, I could have let myself shed some self-pitying tears and justified some sort of sugar binge or other irrational response.

Instead, I took action. While it wasn't in my cards to leave for Hawaii the next day, I was able to clear my schedule for the following weekend and book a massage. Then I made a list of other nurturing activities I could enjoy and promised myself I would not turn my computer or my iPad on even once for the whole weekend. That would at least create a much needed mini-staycation. Suddenly my mood lifted and my energy level shot up as if rocket propelled."

So how do you learn to monitor yourself? Honestly, with a lot of practice. Start by trying to do it when you're not under a lot of pressure, say around the house on a weekend. If you live with a lot of other people and lead a busy life, it will be more difficult to learn, but it can be done. You can't will yourself to have these micro-thoughts—they always happen when you're thinking about something else. The trick is to notice a shift in your mood, which is what you're looking for. Our minds are constantly meandering off track all day long, and pleasant diversions like anticipating some fun event in the future are not what you're looking for. **You want to notice the stray thoughts that trigger *negative* emotions, that begin the downward spiral.** Anything can trigger them—a song on the radio, something said on TV, a comment from a family member, cleaning out a drawer and finding an old letter—the trigger doesn't matter, it's your *response* that does.

Here are some more examples:

- A question from your boss about a report you're working on sparks micro-thoughts about your over-burdened schedule, which triggers feelings of inadequacy and anger at yourself for not being better at time management. These feelings attach themselves to the report, so you become even more resistant to finishing it, and by the time you finally force yourself to complete it, the project has become a hateful, stressful experience. When in truth, it was just a fairly simple report you could have knocked out in a few hours.
- A friend meets you for a drink after work wearing an expensive new dress. She looks vibrant and attractive and ready for whatever life places on her plate. Your first reaction is to be happy for her, as she appears relaxed and confident. Then you focus on her new dress and smile because the lavender color is so flattering to her dark blue eyes. But then you suddenly feel the need for a second drink and you make it a double, as you sense your mood heading south. Why? Because you compared yourself to your friend and came up wanting. Even though *she* didn't do or say anything that upset you, your own micro-response set off a chain reaction. First you were envious because your friend has managed to maintain a significant weight loss, while you struggle daily and have never reached your goal weight. So you beat yourself up about it and your self-esteem plummeted. Second, you wish you could afford some new clothes, but you're still paying off debts from when you were unemployed last year. You see how this is going—**when you measure your life by what's *not* happening, by what you *don't***

have, you'll never be happy. However, if you can capture those micro-thoughts and understand why you're suddenly sad, you can do something about it. You can refocus on what *is* working in your life right now and magnify that. And you can take action to finally reach your own goals, rather than stare wistfully at others who have met theirs.

By now, we've all heard many times that our thoughts are creative, but we need to realize that **our micro-thoughts also create our reality**. And they are potentially more dangerous if we are unaware of them. Learning to witness your own reactions, your own passing ideas and thoughts can be one of the most powerful life tools you develop. If you want to make a serious effort at attaining this skill, here are some suggestions:

1. Obsessively keep a journal of one entire day. This will have to be a day off from normal life. Set a timer to record your mood every 15 minutes. Each entry can be short: *did laundry, feeling good, whistled a happy tune.* If you start to see a downward trend, examine your recent thoughts and try and identify the triggers. If you can't recall, then set your timer for shorter and shorter increments. The goal is to become aware of the triggering thought the **instant** it shoots across your mind, so you can choose a different emotional reaction to it.

2. Look for patterns in your negative micro-thoughts. Do similar situations cause more of them? Do certain people stimulate them? Are you more apt to have them at certain times of the day? Answering these kinds of questions helps you increase your awareness.

3. If you need visual support, post reminders in key spots to keep you on the lookout. Note To Self: my response is ALWAYS my choice.

Of course we aren't going to stop having negative thoughts. There are even times when they could be called for. What you do want, though, is to be in charge of how you *react* to your negative thoughts. Assign them a different sort of power—the ability to inspire deeper self-examination and the ability to fuel personal growth. That way, a negative thought can instantly be transformed into a good thing. **And that is pure alchemy of the highest order.**

We know what you're thinking—this sounds tough to master. Yes, it could be, nut most things worth learning are. Raise your hand if you agree. We're waiting. There. That wasn't so difficult, was it?

**Cool Tool**

Try wearing a Positivity Bracelet to remind yourself to monitor your mood. (Make one or find them online.) Wear one to maintain your own positive focus and pass some others onto pals. There are several ways to use them, and one idea is to move the bracelet from one wrist to the other and back again throughout the day as you observe your negative thoughts and replace them with something more positive. Of course a rubber band would work, but gets fewer style points.

"Happiness is a choice. The more happiness you choose, the more life presents you with experiences to feel happy about."
~Janice Jumpingforjoy

MIKE CONTINUES:

"One thing I further developed in the circus was a strong work ethic. I had to practice hard every day, always trying to improve, always learning new skills. You can't afford to remain static or rest on what you did yesterday…what new thing can you do today? All these circus performers had an incredible work ethic, and I see that element missing from a lot of people's lives today. So many people are looking for the easy way out, the fast ticket, overnight success. Adding more joy to your life takes a similar dedication. How badly do you want to be happier? Then devote that much effort into realizing your goal."

Even though he's a hyper happy guy, Mike is still very disciplined in what he does to maintain his perky outlook on life. **He has a series of happiness practices he does, such as:**

- ☺ Weather permitting, he does earthing (no, not mooning, look it up!)
- ☺ He continues to devour books and articles on happiness and mindful living.
- ☺ He travels all over the world to take—and teach—courses on personal growth in an endless loop of inspiration.
- ☺ He's a joy-seeking magnet, consciously spending a significant part of each day hanging out where other joy-filled people are enjoying their lives.
- ☺ He plays with his food: makes faces on pancakes, draws cartoons on bananas, adds nasturtiums to his salads, just because it amuses his daughter (and himself in the process).

Make **Joy Jars** to hold ideas you can grab and implement right away, such as:
- happy quotes
- love notes
- notes of encouragement from one family member to another
- ideas for FUN days and vacations
- Then anytime anyone in the house needs a lift, they reach in and see what they get. Kind of like a happiness bank or a tarot of joy, and these happy prompts move our ideas from your head into action.

Get out of the house! Now.

Seriously, take this book with you, but go outside—unless of course there's a blizzard or something, then never mind. But don't be a wimp and let a little rain keep you inside. It's just water. You probably won't melt. When Oriana lived on the Oregon coast where it gets really stormy in the winter and can rain for weeks at a time *without ever stopping*, she bought a rainsuit (yep, that's what it's called) and tall rubber boots and just went walking on the beach every day anyway. Guess what? That's when all the super cool stuff washes ashore, when other people are splayed out on couches watching people have fun on

TV. And there are even more benefits than agates and sand dollars, lovely as those are.

According to a study at the University of Kansas, **people who spent three days in nature had a 50% increase in performance on creativity tests.** Even just looking at nature works! Other studies proved that people who live in rooms with views of nature (as opposed to the back of a convenience store) are better able to focus on tasks, handle life's challenges and are seriously happier. And our indoor-centric kids are spending less and less time outdoors and suffering the consequences. The next time your son asks for a new techno toy, give him a badminton set instead—and show him how to use it. He might even grow to like it. It could happen.

This website: www.beoutthere.org is a great resource. Sadly, today kids aged 8-18 spend 53 hours a week indoors consuming entertainment media! Only 6% will play outside on their own without the sole of mom's foot shoving them out.

Sure, some people are dedicated city dwellers who find the outdoors a bit scary and uncomfortable. Yes, there are more bugs and other animal companions, and the only AC you'll have is the shade of a tree or a breeze off the water—but **your brain responds to nature in profound ways**. A better memory. Enhanced thinking and creativity. Relaxation, less stress. Especially after a few days of techno-freedom, your brain can return to a primordial state of well-being. It's the Big Cosmic Ahhhh.

Mike knows even a walk in the park can help, and he prefers to go barefoot. Perhaps most surprising, simply looking at photos of nature induces better performance on mental tests. Toward that end, we've made some pretty virtual visits for you to add to your computers as wallpaper. But they aren't a substitute for the real, mossy, greeny, toe-tickling thing. So go outside, already. What are you waiting for? Go immerse yourself in some joyful fresh air. Remember when we were kids and all we had to play with was outside?

Live in harmony with your world Think about it—how deeply do you live on this planet?

- ♣ know the phase of the moon, commune with it…have a full moon picnic
- ♣ reflect the season in your home…a basket of bright fall leaves on your desk sets an aromatic mood
- ♣ get outside and touch the earth—go barefoot, go wading, get out the slip 'n slide
- ♣ start a collection of shells or fossils or unicorn horns (the fun is in the searching)

Happit: *naturing* **Bring the outside in every day.** For 21 days without interruption, go outside and choose at least one object to bring home. (Preferably not roadkill.) It can be a pine cone from your yard, a crow feather you find on the sidewalk, a colorful stone you trip over. What it is or where you collect it is not the real point—it's getting outside and paying closer attention to your environment that matters most. Extra credit for making a work of art out of all 21 objects at the end of the three weeks. For even more fun, involve kids or friends…have a scavenger hunt. Or go for 26 days and look for things that reflect every letter of the alphabet: apple, bone, cone, daffodil, echinacea, feather, and so on. (Make up your own rule for X!)

☺ Enjoy more primal experiences, especially if you're a city dweller: gather wood, build a fire and cook over it; sleep under the stars and study the night sky; grow some food; observe and foster wildness in nature. (Spider webs don't count.) Stop living from the neck up! **Go native!** Build a shelter from wind fallen branches, driftwood, palm fronds…whatever is there and spend a night in it…it's the *Survivor* experience. You'll appreciate your comfy life more afterwards.

Lift the corners of your mouth

Did all that fresh air make you smile? It's a scientifically proven fact—really, go look it up—even pretending to smile can make you feel happier. Even wilder, sticking a pen in your mouth sideways so that it forces your facial muscles to start a smile lights up the happy place in your brain! (Someone got paid to figure that out.) Smiling for real, well that's even better—it gets those smiley faced endorphins on a roll. As some sage once noted: if you aren't using your smile, you're like someone with a million dollars in the bank and no checkbook! There are thousands of languages in the world, yet there is one thing that is understood everywhere: a smile. There must be an evolutionary reason why we all instinctively shape our mouths in that universal sign. We're automatically drawn to people who are smiling, in fact it's contagious, so it makes sense that **more good things accrue to people who spend more time smiling.**

Research shows that smiling even when you don't really mean it DOES improve your mood. Smiling somehow tricks your mind into believing you really are happy. Smiling is also relaxing and boosts your immune system, plus it lowers your blood pressure and releases endorphins (natural pain killers). How cool is that?

Happit: *smiling* **Make yourself smile every time you think of it all day long.** (It works better if you smile *at* someone, though the dog will work in a pinch. Not so sure about a goldfish.) You don't have to know the nice people or even like them, just grin anyway. Do not let one day go by without smiling for 21 days in a chirpy row. Smile at everyone, you never know who's an angel, or the Fairy Godmother you're about to meet. We live in a circular world: every smile you give away, every word of encouragement you offer, enriches your own life in full return. Be prepared to be bowled over like a teetering pin blasted by a Brunswick purple/blue Nexus ball when you see how people react to you once you master this happit. A smile is a curve that sets everything straight, and a smiling person brings happiness wherever they go.

> "Be the smile you wish to see in the world...
> and create more   happiness." ~Dr. Happy

> "A smile is the light in your window that tells others there is a caring, sharing person inside." ~Denis Waitley

Where's your funny bone?

(It's more than bumping your humerus bone.) Make a study of what amuses you and makes you laugh—then seek it out often and make it easily available. Spend more time with friends who make you laugh—and who laugh at your humor, too. You'll create a circle of laughter together if you find each other funny. According to many studies, laughter is practically a miracle cure for many of our 21st century stress-induced ailments.

Throw a Laughfest: invite friends to bring their favorite comedy albums or YouTube clips or movie excerpts and share them. Discuss… how do you view comedy differently? Why? A great way to discover new sources of laughter and deepen relationships.

Put humor on display: load your coffee table with joke books, cartoon collections and so on to encourage guests to dip into them and share what they find amusing.

Learn to tell a good joke: the ability to make people laugh is a skill to cherish.

Pick a ring tone that makes a joyful noise: that way you smile every time you answer your phone. (Smiles can be *heard* by the way.) It's an old telemarketing trick—if you smile while speaking on the phone you'll come across much better.

Spend more time with playful animals: get down on the floor with them. How does the world look from their point of view? Now we're having fun, aren't we?

Take a 5-year-old on an outing: experience the zoo or circus or a park through her eyes. What have you forgotten about having fun?

Laugh when you can, apologize when you should, and let go of what you can't change. Life's too short to be anything...but happy. Happiness is what we're made of.

☺ **Have you heard about laughter yoga?** Founded in 1995 in India by Dr. Madan Kataria, laughter yoga is used therapeutically in schools, cancer wards, prisons, nursing homes and local community colleges. To learn more, visit www.laughteryoga.org

> "Laughter is the sun that drives winter from the human face."
> ~Victor Hugo

☺ To cause others to smile and laugh is a joy worth giving yourself. All day long ask: Will this make me FEEL good? If the answer is no, do something different.

> "The most wasted of all days is one without laughter."
> ~ e.e. cummings

An overlooked aspect of fun is appreciating the value of **whimsy** in your home, office and daily life—stop being so darn serious! If you must view life as a school, at least let it be recess once in awhile. Surround yourself with things that make you smile and laugh—whether or not your neighbors or your Aunt Sally approve. Go ahead and collect whirligigs…you know you want to! Or velvet Elvises or pink flamingoes or whatever tickles you. Want to relive your youth? Collect memorabilia that was popular then. Have you secretly always wanted a tiki bar in your basement? Go for it! Who cares if it's not HGTV-worthy?

Top of the list

Mike is betting you can't guess what's reported to be the number one contributor to happiness. According to *The Journal of Personality and Social Psychology,* it all comes down to autonomy—the feeling that you are in charge of your life and your fate. Whether or not you identify as the controlling sort, feeling like you have some measure of control over the key elements of your life provides the greatest boost to your joy. All you have to do is think of situations where you have little or no control to realize how true this is.

From our point of view, the most important point we want to make in this chapter is that **it's all your choice** to do these steps, try these ideas, change your attitude. **Taking control of your happiness level is the ideal route to enhancing your sense of autonomy.**

AFFIRMATIONS: I immerse myself in joy. I am willing to release my old, limiting ideas, and I no longer have any use for negativity in my life. All I seek now is positive input, and I enjoy each appearance it makes in my life. I make a conscious decision to rejoice every day, even days when I don't want to. Everything has an upside, and I am determined to find it—always.

> "Celebrate endings—for they precede new beginnings."
> ~J. L. Huie

In the next chapter…
In a tasty, nutty shell, you're going to see your future. We'll guide you to envision the panoramic scope of Your Big Happy Life and give you lots of tools to help you visualize your full potential. Hint: it's vast!

Chapter Four
What Do You Really Want?
   envisioning your big happy life

In this chapter:
- ✓ Your meaning of life
- ✓ There's lots of value to be noticed
- ✓ Stop working
- ✓ You are never too old
- ✓ Who are you *now*?
- ✓ Understanding "no"
- ✓ You need a bug list (nothing creepy/crawly)
- ✓ It's not your mom's fault after all
- ✓ What have you got to over-deliver?
- ✓ What do you see?
- ✓ Looking back
- ✓ Sign on the dotted line

**"To succeed in life, you need three things:
a wishbone, a backbone and a funny bone." ~Reba McEntire**

Can you see Your Big Happy Life?
In the last chapter you learned about full joy immersion, and if you gave it a whirl, you discovered the size of the gap between how much happiness you want in your life and how much is already present. So let's spend some time thinking about your long-term happiness. Because you're reading this book, we figure you're someone who wants to get the most out of life, someone who's not content to mosey along the Path of Least Resistance. Nope, not you. You're motivated! You've got ambitions, desires, dreams—though you may be a little short in the Making-Them-Come-True Department. That's okay, we can help with that, but first let's get clear on what you really want.

You might be just starting out in life, wandering down life's byways wondering which of 656 options to choose. Or you might be having a mid-life crisis, feeling like your dreams for yourself are unfulfilled. Or you might be edging toward your third act, ready to reinvent yourself all over again. **Whatever your story, it can have the same ending—getting to thrive, getting to live Your Big Happy Life.** Throughout this chapter we'll be offering lots of different ways for you to envision and design Your Big Happy Life. We don't expect you to do them all…just try some that resonate with you.

"Failing to plan is planning to fail." ~Effie Jones

"Without leaps of imagination or dreaming, we lose the excitement of possibilities. Dreaming, after all, is a form of planning." ~Gloria Steinem

What's the meaning of your life?
One proven route to more happiness is to **identify what adds more meaning to your life.** Discover what you really, truly care about

and do that more often. More singing and less nagging. More art and less thwart. Pulling more weeds and pulling less overtime. **Your passions have power.** Most of us have to work for a living, and even if you don't, read on, because you'll still find relevance in understanding the potential value of your passions. **Most people would welcome an extra stream of income—especially if it comes in from doing something they're wild about.**

Whatever vision you see for your life, working toward goals that get you there ups your happiness. It doesn't matter whether your goal is to switch to a more fulfilling career, to get married and build a family life, to go zip-lining in New Zealand or to simply add more delight to your days. Making steady progress and achieving your desires is deeply satisfying. (And the tougher the goal is to attain, the more pride and joy may ensue.) Or not. We're all different, and isn't that nifty?

☺ Being happier is a life skill you can learn and master. It's not some elusive bluebird that you have to sit in a tree waiting for. Happiness isn't something that just lands on your front porch one day. You can't order it from a catalog, borrow it from a pal or buy it on eBay. It's something you must plant and nurture.

Happit: *values* Make a list of your most cherished values, things that add meaning to your life. What values do you aspire to live by? What values cause you to do or *not do* certain things? For example, some of Mike's core values are: Fun, Friendship, Integrity, Spontaneity, Love, Sincerity, Passion, Honesty, Truth, Accomplishment. **Add at least one new value to your list every day for 21 days.** By the end of that time, thinking about your values (and consciously integrating them into your life) will become second nature. For instance, remembering that you value *spontaneity* can make you more apt to say yes to fun adventures rather than perpetuating old workaholic habits. *Elephant riding in*

Thailand? Sure! Does your life reflect your values? If not, what needs to change?

Work as play, play as work
    One thing wise people have said for ages is: don't just like what you do—***but LOVE* what you do.** The *follow your bliss* prescription. Everyone talks about it because it so darn true—but how many people really reach that level? Have you? As much as bliss is part of the formula, research shows there are other qualities that cause people to love their work, including: creativity, autonomy, mastery, making a difference and being appreciated. As Malcolm Gladwell revealed in *Outliers*, putting in your 10,000 hours to master something is a game changer. What are you willing to devote that much energy to?

        "Be so good they can't ignore you." ~Steve Martin

        "Find a job you like and you add five days to every week."
        ~H. Jackson Browne

MIKE ON *NOT* WORKING:
    "**You Don't Need A Job.** You need to be in love. **I've NEVER had a job!** All I've ever done is what revved me up at that point in my life. **Anyone can earn money, but can you earn money doing what you do for fun?** If you ever took a class, earned a degree or pursued a career to please someone else, then you know the pain of getting sidetracked on someone else's train. **When you can't tell the difference between fun and work, you know you've found your heart's mission.** When you wake up on Saturday and can't wait to 'work' on your special project, you know you're on the right track."

        "Nothing great was ever achieved without enthusiasm."
        ~ Ralph Waldo Emerson

"Choose a job you love, and you will never have to work a day in your life." ~Confucius

Create a Joy List for yourself—what makes you happy? What hobbies engage you? What would you do for free if you could? How could you get paid for doing that? Don't filter anything out, lock up your adult inner critic. You never know which silly little thing will spark an idea. These passion points can lead you to new career paths or to additional income or simply point you toward renewed ways to add more fun back into your life.

Mike knows a wacky guy who's made a fortune selling plans to make your own potato gun! Really, that's no joke. One of Mike's early business mentors started a million dollar company by growing alfalfa sprouts in his bathtub. Another fellow earns a huge income selling the tools to make wire jewelry and another guy with a passion for ancient warfare sells historically accurate weapons and suits of armor. All things that at first glance do NOT sound like profitable career paths, but they absolutely are!

Most adults lose sight of what they use to enjoy, and often there are great clues there to what you might still enjoy. Oriana is somewhat exercise-resistant (at least in the traditional, go-to-the-gym sense of it), but when she recalled a childhood passion for Napoleon Dynamite (one of Mike's favorite movies) style tetherball, she found a place to play that whenever she likes. It's great form of exercise that doesn't feel like exercise because it's FUN!

Reviewing your Joy List reminds you to keep developing your vision for Your Big Happy Life. It also increases the likelihood that you'll actually make it happen.

Happit: *playing* Reinstate more play in your life! It's surefire way to turn back you mental age clock. Borrow some kids if you have to in order to get in the mood. If you enjoyed playgrounds as a kid, find an adult version: a parcourse or fitness trail outfitted with fun exercise equipment along the way. How about a class in dancing with your dog, or training your dog for agility competitions? Have you heard of Frisbee golf? Buy a hula hoop! Or go into a big toy store and see what cool things kids have to choose from today. Get out and play catch with your kids. Borrow your daughter's scooter. Were you a Nancy Drew fan? Try geocaching, a fun activity that combines orienteering and detective work to find hidden prizes all over the world. Do this daily for those powerful, brain-training 21 days, then ask yourself how these activities might inform your vision for Your Big Happy Life.

☺ If you don't like where you are, then change it. You are not a tree.

MIKE TALKS MORE HAPPY:
"This is one of my biggest secrets ever: All my life I've had hundreds of people ask me: **How can I have more fun and how can I be funnier?** I observe people differently from most people, and I've always been intensely fascinated by watching little kids. I love to watch them jumping around, uninhibited. When you're a child, your only job is to have fun! They don't worry about anything, they don't care what people think of their actions. So I adopted that attitude, too, and I don't ever worry about what someone else will think of me. In fact, a wise teacher has said: *What you think of me is none of my business.* Good words to live by.

Another way children behave is spontaneously. They don't edit themselves or second guess their ideas. Kids live in the moment and set any worries aside. I learned that when I'm spontaneous I achieve the most amazing things. If you want to live a magical, Big Happy Life, be more like a kid."

Get out some Tinker Toys
What gave you joy as a kid, can bring you joy as an adult. **Make a list of all the things you can remember enjoying throughout your**

childhood, regardless of your age at the time. There's often a deep level of happiness that can be mined and restored to your life from those memories. When Oriana was young she knit ill-fitting sweaters for her terrier. Now she sews better fitting Halloween costumes for her spoodle —with just as much pleasure. (There could even be a new career in that.) But some things never change: she's still looking for good domino and scrabble players. Mike can still bust a move on a unicycle or stroll down the sidewalk upside down (walking on his hands…he doesn't levitate).

How about a reinvention?
One of the positive upshots of an economic meltdown is that some people are inspired—or forced—to become entrepreneurial and create their own livelihoods, often turning their passions into profits. People are much happier and earning great livings…
- Leading medieval history tours in Europe
- Developing iPad apps and goofy games for your cat
- Testing ratatouille recipes and blogging about them
- Recycling icky french fry waste into biofuel
- Running fantasy football leagues

"One must have the adventurous daring to accept oneself as a bundle of possibilities and undertake the most interesting game in the world: making the most of one's best." ~H. E. Fosdick

"Dwell in possibility." ~Emily Dickinson

If there's something you care deeply about, there are probably lots of other people who share that interest and would pay for expertise in that niche. **So what are you good at?** You probably have a clue what your Number One Passion is. It may well not be anything you think you could turn into a career. Think again. **Start researching how you can get paid to do what you'd do for free.** Search online, look for blogs that are monetized (either with paid ads or by selling products). Search keyword phrases related to your passion and study the results pages in Google—if there are a bunch of paid ads on the side of the page, that's a sign there's money to be made in that niche. Take a minute to jot down one dream you'd hate to die without doing.

> "There are many things in life that will catch your eye, but only a few of these will catch your heart. Pursue those."
> ~Michael Knollin

> "Life is not easy for any of us. But what of that? We must have perseverance and above all confidence in ourselves. We must believe we are gifted for something."
> ~Marie Curie

A slightly different question is: What's your core talent? What's the one thing you're known for, the thing that comes easily to you, the thing where you shine the brightest? For Mike it's making people laugh. For Oriana it's integrating words and images. Some other examples are: organizing, logistics, teaching, inventing new products, empathy, making connections for people and mentoring.

By joining your passion with your talent you may discover new areas of endeavor to consider.
- A passion for European culture + a core talent for teaching = becoming an itinerant ESL teacher living throughout Europe.
- A passion for being with children + a core talent for organizing = running a summer camp or planning kids' birthday parties.
- A passion for vegetable gardening + core talent of logistics = designing free community garden spaces all over town.

We urge—*nag*—you to start journaling about this process if you haven't already. The great thing about a private journal is you feel emboldened to state your wildest ideas and biggest dreams. There should be no restraints on your vision as you record your thoughts—no editing allowed! In fact, studies show that **writing down goals with your hand**

creates more of a direct conduit from your brain, because it stimulates the reticular activating system (RAS) we spoke of in Chapter Two. The RAS filters what your brain processes, giving more importance to what you're actively focusing on—something the physical act of writing brings to the forefront. The RAS then signals your cerebral cortex to pay attention, to remember those ideas. After you write down your goals, your brain works overtime to help you achieve them, by showing you signs and signals that match your desires.

Happit: *shining* **Do something daily that uses your core talent.** If you're stumped, ask other people what they think your core talent is. Rather than trying to get better at things you dislike, why not focus on what you excel at? How do you want to star in your life? Start a simple tracking system and make sure you do at least one thing daily for 21 days that engages your most significant talent. Extra credit if others see and notice you doing it, but it's really about spending your time in ways that *you* find fulfilling. *Work doesn't have to be work!*

> **"Words can rush out in their raw, feral state when the pen is your tool." ~Patrick McLean**

> **"It's very important to set the rules in your favor. You do not have to follow what everyone else is doing." ~Tim Ferris**

Intention meets opportunity and leaps to life
    Even though he attained his first big dream of joining the circus while still a teenager, Mike had even bigger goals, and he didn't waste much time aiming for those, either.

MIKE GETS HAPPY:
    "Ever since I was in tenth grade I always thought I could have a TV show, and I would even admit that dream whenever someone asked me what I wanted to do with my life. (Though of course no one ever

took me seriously or thought I could do it.) As exciting as Ringling Brothers was, I always saw it as a stepping stone to having my own show. Not long after leaving the circus, I had settled back in Indiana, and I got a phone call out of the blue from a local TV station manager asking me if I wanted to audition for a new kid's show they were creating.

In my belief system, however, it wasn't really out of the blue, because **the call matched up with an intention I set for myself years earlier**, an intention I focused on in an ongoing effort to place myself at the intersection of preparation and opportunity. Someone who knew my history suggested me as a possible host, so the call was really a result of my networking and letting people know my background and my desires. *Did I want to audition?* Do clowns wear funny noses? Were my shoes size 28?

They wanted to see me the very next day, and they wanted me to come dressed as a hobo character. I called my sister—and thank goodness for her—because she sewed me a costume on the spot. So the next day at my audition they told me to give them five or six minutes of my best material. The director said, "Pretend there's a big audience of kids here and be as funny as possible." I'd never auditioned in front of cameras or for any TV show, so I was kind of freaked out. I did my best, but I couldn't tell how it was going over. At the end of it, the owner of this conglomerate of regional stations thanked me and said: 'We'll give you a call…we still have several days of auditions to go.'

I felt in my heart that wasn't a good sign, that it was a brush-off, that I hadn't managed to impress them. **So I decided I absolutely had to do something radically different to change their minds right then and there.** I was certainly not going to come so close to my dream and walk away in defeat without making a Herculean effort. When I went back to the lobby I saw the young receptionist sitting there, so I decided to entertain *her.* I figured if I could make her laugh and smile, then she might go back and say: *You need to hire this guy.* So I asked her if anyone else had juggled and she said not much, so I grabbed my juggling balls and just showed her every trick I could think of. Then I picked up a chair and balanced it on my head and then a flower pot on my nose and anything I could find just to get her laughing.

So while I was still there doing every crazy thing I could think of, the owner and manager came out. They watched me interacting with their receptionist and saw some of the bigger tricks I was doing. The next thing I knew, they were conferring again, then the owner came over to me and said to forget about waiting for a phone call. For a second I misunderstood and thought they were telling me to go home, and my heart sank to my knees. But then he stuck out his hand and told me **I was hired** and to show up Monday morning!

In that very instant I could see all my preparation, all my hard work, all my intense study coming together to create my new reality. I knew absolutely that this was the beginning of my whole new life, reaching an even bigger dream. I tried to be professional and not overreact in front of them, but as soon as I got outside and away from the station I let out this enormous, loud yelp of victory. I started dancing around, whooping and screaming, jumping up and down, just going nuts with excitement. I think I even did a flip. **I knew my star was on the rise."**

☺ **What's at your intersection?** If you gaze into our crystal ball, what do you see yourself doing at your intersection of preparation and opportunity? What have you been preparing for—perhaps even without an endgame in mind? Will you recognize opportunity when it comes calling? Or are you ready to go and track it down yourself? What's the point of being alive if you don't at least try to do something remarkable? Happiness is a choice. The more happiness you choose, the more life presents you with experiences to feel happy about. And isn't that a nice victory circle?

Do you know what NO really means?
Before you finish defining Your Big Happy Life, take a quick look backward and be sure you haven't left some key dreams by the roadside. Dreams that were perhaps run over by other people who never had a license to stifle your ambitions, and certainly not to leave them for dead. Are there times when you took *no* for your answer that you wish you could change? What can you learn from those experiences? Are there former goals you'd like to resurrect? **Mike instinctively knew that *no* actually has many possible meanings, including:**
- yes, but not now
- yes, but with reservations
- yes, but with conditions
- maybe later
- maybe, if you get more training or experience
- maybe, after all options have been considered
- we don't think you're really interested
- we misunderstand your qualifications or position
- we need more references
- you and/or your idea are fine, but you may need to look elsewhere

Because Mike did not hear *No, forget it, go home, we don't want you*, he remained at the TV station and persisted toward his goal, making it up as he went along. He listened to his gut, which told him not to leave, to make an even BIGGER effort.

And he got a MUCH bigger result!

One way to apply this lesson when faced with objections and potential negative responses is to ask or find out *why not*? **The key is to transform *no* from a refusal into an obstacle to be overcome.** If you can deal with the obstacle, then you can probably change the *no* to a *yes*. Mike felt his obstacle was that the bosses weren't choosing him because they didn't realize the full scope of his abilities. He figured if he could find a way to better demonstrate to them that he *was* the right man for the job, then they would pick him. Wouldn't you pick the guy with a flower pot on his nose?

On the road of life, *no* is not a dead end—it's a detour. Some of us are more easily demoralized and slink away from the slightest whiff of rejection. Getting a *no* isn't necessarily a reflection of you or your ideas—it may just be bad timing or that your idea doesn't mesh with their needs. Regroup, alter your plan and keep trying. People who quit cannot succeed. It's that simple.

On the other hand, *no* can be a useful test of conviction. What you think you want does not always turn out to be the best path for you. Facing rejection can force you to be sure you're on the best course. If you believe you are, then keep going. Otherwise, make some adjustments. Rosie O'Donnell famously tells everyone who asks her advice: *Do NOT to go into show business*, because she knows if one voice of rejection deters someone, then they'll never succeed in that crazy biz. When you do get a *no,* if it makes you want to fight even harder to barge past it, then you're on the right path.

"It isn't a calamity to die with dreams unfulfilled, but it is a calamity not to dream." ~Benjamin Mays

☺ It's not who you are that holds you back, it's who you think you aren't.

"Happiness is not a mystery, it's a work ethic. You have to train your brain to be positive just like you work out your body." ~Shawn Achor

"Follow your heart. It knows exactly where to take you." ~Cheryl Richardson

Are you sure you know what you want?

Are you, really? For Mike, this was an epic oops, because he hadn't yet learned how to refine his goals. It's a good thing he was young and energetic, or he would never have been able to pull this off.

MIKE CONFIDES:

"I was hired to play a character who already existed, called Happy the Hobo. The show was to be called *Happy's Place*, and I thought it was just going to be a Saturday morning show, probably a half hour. So when I showed up the first day, the station owner and manager sat me down and told me they were actually planning a Monday through Friday show. So suddenly my job grew five-fold! And before I could wrap my mind around how I was going to fill five half-hour shows a week, they added, 'Wait, it gets even better! We're going to bring back the live kids shows that were so popular in the 1950s and '60s…we want you to do a **90-minute live show five days a week!**'

Well I was totally freaking out over that news, but I spoke up and said I'd been able to write a lot of my own routines for Ringling, and I'd love to help hire the writers for the new show. That got a laugh, because they told me they wanted me to **do all the writing**, too! So then I was COMPLETELY wigged out…it just seemed way too ambitious for me to create seven and a half hours of television every week all by myself. But before I could adjust to all of that, they piled on another thing—they told me they were going to bring in a live audience of kids. So then I was just way, way out, a thousand miles out of my comfort zone. **I was a good juggler, but that was a LOT of moving objects to keep in the air at once.**

So they took me into a big empty room and said, "Here's another exciting thing—this is your new set." And I said, *Where*? And they pointed to a blank blue wall and told me I got to "interact with it" and got to design and develop the look of the show along with my character and everything else.

Now for a seasoned TV professional with a big staff and plenty of time and a decent budget to play with, that would be enormously empowering and wonderful to undertake. I didn't have any of that.

So I'm certain that **when the show debuted, it was the ugliest TV show in history**, because it was just me and the blue wall for the first two weeks. I knew nothing—zero, nada—about special effects or working with a camera, and even my crew wasn't much help because they'd never done a kid's show either. And my bosses just told me to "be funny, to do some of that juggling." And I'm like: *for 90 minutes a day!?* So they said I could show some cartoons, but that still left lots and lots of time to fill.

One joke, one stunt at a time, I got through it. I developed recurring bits and gathered props. Over time I added a chair, then a mailbox and a little tree and gradually the set began to turn into a playful, colorful space. I ended up with a character who was part Bozo, part Letterman, part Benny Hill—half circus clown and half stand-up comic.

The irony is, instead of working my way up to that level of air time and responsibility, **my entire television career was plopped in my lap all at once as one gigantic creative challenge.** Oh yeah, and I was also one of the producers for the whole eight years I was on the air, which meant I also had to figure out the logistics for the crazy things we eventually did. **Proving that ignorance is bliss, because I didn't know it couldn't be done, I just did it."**

"All glory comes from daring to begin."
~Alexander Graham Bell

"Impossible is just an opinion." ~D. Chopra

What have you told yourself is impossible for you?

**"Life isn't about finding yourself. Life is about creating yourself."
~George Bernard Shaw**

(You can be whomever you want to be…remember how Mike had to create his clown persona in the circus? There's no reason why you can't do the same—but with smaller shoes!)

It's a good thing Mike was not easily daunted and didn't lose sight of the fact that he was living his dream. That first night when he finally went home and wrote down all the things he'd just agreed to do, he was equal parts excited and petrified. From an early age Mike had always written out pro/con lists for any project he began, but that night the con side of the page was definitely longer. Sure, this was his dream, but he didn't want to fall flat on his face (even if he did position the banana peel). Still, **the only thing between him and his Big Happy Life was a lot of hard work** doing exactly what he loved to do—so he went for it wholeheartedly.

And just to make it even crazier, for the first six months they had him doing a Saturday show, too! But after awhile he had to draw the line on that one…even Mike Fry couldn't keep up with ten hours of content every week.

"I am always doing things I can't do…
that's how I get to do them." ~Pablo Picasso

"Success is getting what you want.
Happiness is wanting what you get." ~Dave Gardner

On a clear day you can see your future
Don't overlook negatives as part of your information gathering process. **Write a Bug List:** list nine things about your life that bug you, make you unhappy or that you wish you could change soon. Why just nine? Because it's an irritating number! We are wired to want the

resolution of certain notes in melodies, of certain outcomes in stories and the harmony of certain numbers (and nine is itching to get to ten). **Transforming something on your list might become your new mission in life.** Think of all the crusaders who charge off on their white horses righting wrongs. Does that sound like you?

The other value of a Bug List is to make sure you don't let anything that's on it weasel into Your Big Happy Life. If some of them are already there, then that's your first task—figuring out how to banish them pronto!

MIKE'S STILL TALKING:

"**One big takeaway for me from the experience of getting my TV show, was the importance of having a clear vision for Your Big Happy Life.** Yes, I wanted to do all those things and I wanted to have my own show, but I thought I'd ease into it, grow into it. Instead I got one huge cosmic cherry pie in my face. **The more clarity you have up front, the easier it is to manifest exactly what you want.** If you just have a vague dream of traveling a lot, you can end up driving a school bus. So when you're envisioning your dream, get clear on all parts of it, write it down in great detail. It's so easy to go off track…I like to follow those bright shiny objects, too, but it isn't always the best way to make your dreams come to life. You also have to know what you *don't* want, so you can walk away or turn down aspects that don't really fit into your happy life plan.

If you peeked into my office at *Happy's Place* you would've seen all kinds of positive quotes on the walls and motivational ideas everywhere to keep me on track. I knew I needed all the help I could create for myself to make the show work."

"Nothing is impossible, the word itself says *I'm possible*!"
~Audrey Hepburn

So have you ever manifested more than you were ready for? As you fully develop your plan, be sure you're ready for it to arrive. How clear do you feel you are about what sort of Big Happy Life you'd like to have? The great thing about clarity is it makes the way forward so obvious.

> "Beware what you set your heart upon,
> for it shall surely be yours."
> ~ Ralph Waldo Emerson

MORE MIKE:
"One of the things I fell in love with doing Happy's Place was the joy of accomplishing everything I wanted to do on the show. Early on I became obsessed by goal setting. It was so important to me to achieve my dreams. Right before I was hired to do *Happy's Place* I spent the last money I had on a class in goal setting. During that class **I created a Master List of 167 Life Goals**. Then I made vision boards for key goals. I collected inspirational quotes from famous comedians and posted them all around me.

One of my goals for the show was to learn to make professional music videos, and I often spent weeks learning a song and perfecting what I was going to do with it. Every time I rehearsed a number I made a check mark on my list, until I could check it off entirely as being mastered. That gave me an enormous sense of pride and accomplishment and made me feel really good about the work I was doing. I loved seeing actual progress in my skills and other life goals ticked off on my list."

☺☺☺☺☺☺☺☺☺☺☺☺☺☺☺☺☺☺☺☺☺☺☺☺☺

Happy The Hobo Highlights
Mike continued to prove what Art Linkletter learned earlier—kids really do say the darndest things on live TV. Case in point:
Happy The Hobo (to a young boy with a concerned expression): *What's your name?*
Boy who shall remain nameless: *I hafta go pee.*

Popular bit: "Okay, I need one boy and one girl for today's hula hoop contest. Everybody stand up and practice. Hips to the right, hips to the left. Baboom!" The kids convulse in laughter as Happy pretends he's thrown his hip out.

A strange love child: "I never wanted Happy's Place to be just a kid's show. I've never thought of myself as Just a Mr. Rogers…I'm more a cross between Bozo the clown and David Letterman."

Visits from Zookeepers: Unbeknownst to the handler, this cockatoo's wing feathers had grown out enough to take flight…which he did, making quite a trip around the TV studio. Of course the kids just thought it was part of the act. Mike recalls: "When people talked to me about animals they saw on the show, I hoped they learned something or gained a sense of appreciation for animals. And that made me happy, too."

☺☺☺☺☺☺☺☺☺☺☺☺☺☺☺☺☺☺☺☺☺☺☺☺☺☺☺☺☺

"The true value of any goal is how aiming for it shapes you."
~Someone Wise

MIKE REMEMBERS BEING HAPPY

"What did I enjoy the most? The live audience, getting to be totally spontaneous and the immediacy of the feedback. I created the content and had full control of it because I produced it, and then I got immediate laughs THAT day. I got a special kick out of the parents. They sat off-camera and it was fun to make them laugh, too. Parents sometimes laughed even harder than the kids. I never considered it to be just a kids show, but more of a family show. The demographics of the audience was in fact mixed, which was highly unusual. Nielsen & Arbitron said we were top 10 in the country in that way…another way I got to be a pioneer. My producer didn't even understand it…he was just concerned with the kids' portion of the audience. He wanted me to teach kids about poetry and art, but I told him I'm not an educator, **I'm an entertainer... I can be silly. That's what I do."**

"Your vision of where or what you want to be is the greatest asset you have. Without having a goal it's difficult to score."
~Paul Arden

"I always wanted to be somebody, but I should have been more specific." ~Lily Tomlin

It's not your mom's fault
Few of us survive childhood unscathed to some degree—that's what growing up is all about—trying new things and failing—going in new directions, with or without mom and dad's permission. At some point we all have to finally let go of any residual blame we're hauling around, excuses we trot out to rationalize why we aren't making our dreams come true. The dance lessons you didn't get, the space camp you couldn't attend, the prom dress disaster you were sure would ruin your life—it's time to release them to that place in the sky where lost wishes go to vaporize. **It's time to accept full and total responsibility for everything that happens in your life.** Mom will be happy, too.

If Mike had been content to let others take control of his show at any point, *Happy's Place* never would have attained the wonderful success it did. Even though he had no idea what he was getting himself into or the monumental amount of work it would take to build a popular show, from the outset Mike was in it to win it. Though his Big Happy Life didn't arrive perfectly packaged in a pretty bow, Mike understood that this would, indeed, become the life he had dreamed about for so long. The whole weight of the show landed squarely on his colorful shoulders: writing, producing, starring, promoting—all of it.

☺There's a reason your eyes are in front of your body...so you can see where you're going, not where you've been. **Affirm:** The past is over and cannot hurt me. I release its hold over me and claim my true power over the only time that matters: this moment, here, now. I live in this new now. This is the only place I can express my power.

"Some people act like their soul mate is a scapegoat."
~Ursula Upbeat

OUT OF MIKE'S MOUTH:
"Running that show taught me a lot about responsibility. At age 22 I was suddenly a co-producer of a TV show, writing 99% of my material, and then I had to work with my director and crew to help them understand my vision for the sketches I wanted to do. If I didn't involve them in the creative process they wouldn't get on board with my zany ideas. All of us were green 20-somethings, and when I took the time to sell my ideas to them, they got involved and cared about my vision too. I accepted full responsibility: it was up to me, I'm the guy, it's my name on the show. Then ultimately I had to sell my ideas to the audience too, because if I didn't get the laughs I'd be in trouble."

Think about your own life. While everyone else is sitting around watching other people's so-called real lives on TV or partying and generally wasting time, what vision of a happier life could you be pursuing? How can you take more ownership of your life, how might you become more action-oriented, how could you make your own life more magical?

MORE MIKE HAPPY TALK:
"When I got the job, I didn't know until the first meeting that I was going to play Happy the Hobo or that the show would be called *Happy's Place*. An interesting fact about Ringling, is that 99% of the clowns have

no stage name…we were the cream of the crop and too cool for that. You didn't want to be known as Bobo the Clown. **But since the goal was to make kids laugh, I decided Happy wasn't such a bad name to be stuck with.** Still, it took me four or five years to completely embrace the name. But, of course, Happy fit me really well, and other people often commented that I *was* a really happy guy. And it turned out to be a great thing to have that aspect of my personality reinforced every day for eight years and beyond. Being called Happy every day became a living, breathing, laughing affirmation."

"What you can do, or think you can, begin it." ~Goethe

☺**Clown Styles:** There are three basic types of clowns: whiteface, auguste and character, which is most often a tramp or hobo. Tramps are sad and down on their luck (Charlie Chaplin made this famous), while hobos are upbeat, fun-loving characters who know everything will turn out all right. Red Skelton's beloved hobo clown character, Freddy the Freeloader, was made famous on his TV show. Makeup for hobo clowns is designed to enhance natural features of the face, never to hide them, and often includes the shadow of new beard growth and a white mouth for contrast.

"Some people dream of success…others stay awake to achieve it." ~Sleepless in Sheboygan

☺**Little known fact:** Right before getting the Happy gig, Mike had been doing stand-up comedy and thought he might pursue that route. And even after he got the show he continued doing stand-up gigs at night—until he started getting recognized as *that Happy guy*, which was just too weird for the vastly different kinds of presentations, so he stopped doing stand-up.

MIKE CONTINUES:

"Another key lesson I learned early in life was to give 110% to what I was doing, to over-deliver. While other people are content to slide by making a 50 or 60% effort, I always knew that the route to real success—and happiness—was to push myself over the top. Even beyond 100%. I was the guy who always stayed later, who was always reading a new motivational book, who spent my own money on cool props, who used what little free time I had to prime my mind to be ever more creative.

One thing that helped was falling in love with personal development books. When reporters came to interview me for the show, they were mystified by all the positive signs and images literally covering my walls. I told them that those were tools I used to work toward success goals, but that kind of attitude was not very common back then.

Even my General Manager was bemused by my enthusiasm. During an early meeting when were discussing ratings I told him **my goal was to have the Number One rated kid's show**. He laughed and said it was valiant of me to want that, but I needed a reality check: *We were an independent station, and it just wasn't possible to compete with the big networks.* I said I think I CAN do it, and I remember leaving there mad, because I wanted him to share my dream, to believe in me. But I didn't let that stop me. In fact, I decided to do everything I could to be successful. **I set a secret goal of having the number one rated kid's show within three years—and I actually hit that goal within about a year and a half.** Ultimately, it was syndicated in 207 cities, and I attribute that success to my devotion to over-delivering every single day.

But wait, there's a bonus: Envisioning a happier tomorrow can actually make you feel happier right now, since your mind is already *there*, being happy."

Happit: *over-delivering* **Find something every day that you can over-deliver on.** It can be small and simple, like adding an index to a report or doing a deeper level of research. Or perhaps you cook a family meal without using any processed foods or sew Susie a sassy Halloween costume—without complaint. Maybe while house sitting for your neighbor you fill her house with flowers for her return. What can you do that's unexpected? How can you add value to your efforts? Would it be worth working half the night to blow your boss away with a snazzy promo video? If it's your usual M.O. to just kinda get by, to fly under the radar, this happit will change all that. **Adopting this happit gets you noticed in a big way**, and can increase your happiness level—IF you enjoy life in the spotlight. Go ahead and see what it's like to be that person who really excels big time. Then after you've tried it, see if it's an authentic fit. If not, that's okay too. Some people prefer a less intense approach to life. If you do enjoy it, then include it in your happy vision. Authenticity trumps everything. Build your happiness visions on the rock of who you really are, Commune with your best self, your highest self, your most authentic version of you. Display your true colors in all their vivid glory.

"Make the most of yourself by fanning the tiny, inner sparks of possibility into flames of achievement." ~Golda Meir

☺ **From a magazine article of the era:** "Happy the Hobo is easily the most recognized person in Fort Wayne, and certainly the most popular, too. His appearances at store openings, parades, company picnics and zoo functions always draw a crowd of squealing youngsters and secretly amused parents. But his show is what really packs 'em in. Happy fans wait up to a year and a half for studio audience tickets."

☺ **Excerpt from newspaper article of the era:** Most people who tune into the show don't realize that Happy is on stage constantly for 90 minutes. While home viewers watch cartoons and commercials, Happy continues to entertain the studio audience. Happy's philosophy is simple but effective: "I try to imagine myself as a kid in the studio and what would make me laugh. I wouldn't like to just sit there during commercial breaks."

"Ordinary people believe only in the possible. Extraordinary people visualize not what is possible or probable, but rather what is impossible. And by visualizing the impossible, they begin to see it as possible." ~Cherie Carter-Scott

"Our deepest wishes are whispers of our authentic selves. We must learn to respect them. We must learn to listen."
~Sarah Ban Breathnach

Could it be magic?
One fun technique (and just a reminder, this is supposed to FUN!) is to engage in some magical thinking and see where it takes you. No, you don't need a wand or a pointy hat, just a willingness to suspend disbelief and a willingness to set aside the laws of physics (or at least Newton's Third Law of Motion).

NOTE: What follows is a guided meditation, which doesn't translate all that well to a printed page, so if you can swing it, have someone else read this to you. Or record it and listen to your own voice.

Find a quiet spot, close your eyes and just imagine your life without rules or consequences, a life without restrictions or obligations, a life where you've accomplished absolutely everything you dreamt up for yourself. You're on top of your game; you're the best at what you do. You adore your life and how you live each day. You are flourishing. You've never been happier. There is perfect flow in your life; everything is in balance and you understand harmony on an intimate level. Notice everything you do during a day. See how it feels to operate at this high level of functioning.

Now the $64,000 question: Exactly what were you doing in this vision? What do you see yourself doing when you don't edit yourself with limitations? Despite whatever real or perceived limits may exist in your life now, if you truly want that life you just witnessed, there's surely a way to reach it.

Mike literally did this when he ran away and joined the circus. Oriana did when she moved out of a big city to live near the ocean in the middle of nowhere, 25 miles from the nearest store. She sacrificed some of her income and a lot of convenience, but she gained precious solitude and endless beaches all to herself.

What ARE you willing to do to create that life? How far are you willing to extend yourself? What will you sacrifice? How badly do you want to make real this vision of Your Big Happy Life? You have to be the one who does the things that other people won't do. That kind of behavior brings the joy and satisfaction of accomplishment. Be an ACTIVE participant in your life, not a passive person who just takes what comes your way. Go out and GRAB what YOU want!

"Don't you ever let a soul in the world tell you that you can't be exactly who you are." ~Lady Gaga (And we would add...or tell you who you want to be.)

You're the star of your life

Having survived high school, it no longer matters whether or not you were chosen for the field hockey team, school plays or the cool kids' clique. Now if you want to play basketball, there's a pick-up game at the park or the Y. If you lean toward theatrics, every town mounts local productions. Just because your desires were dashed once, doesn't mean you can't rekindle ones that still have meaning for you. Go ahead and sparkle!

Stardom for Mike, even as a kids show host, didn't turn out like he thought it would. When he was dreaming up his life as a young man, he thought he wanted to be a TV star, but what that meant changed over time.

MIKE REMEMBERS:

"When I got my TV show and it became a hit, people would say: *Wow, your show is so successful, how does it feel to be a star?* Truthfully, I never thought of myself that way. That was just a by-product. What I wanted was to have the satisfaction of knowing I did my best performance. **All I ever wanted was to make people laugh, to make them happy, to bring some surprise and delight into their day.** That meant everything. I did want to be regarded as an artist at what I did, as someone who cared about my craft as a comedian, But I was just a guy doing what he loved to do.

When I was doing *Happy's Place* there was no internet yet, but **with the advent of Facebook I've reconnected with my fans in a magical way**. It started when my wife Erin came across two women in Australia (of all places) blogging about their childhood in the States, and they recalled being fans of *Happy's Place*. One of them even remembered being at the show in the audience. Then someone else joined in and started to reminisce about being on the show, and more and more people began to comment and share their memories. So Erin added her comment saying that I would love to hear from them. It was her idea to put up a Happy fan page for the show. I thought maybe a few hundred people would find it and enjoy it.

Now there are over 15,000 former fans who hang out on my page: www.Facebook.com/happythehobo . (We hope you're one of them!) Most of them are in their late 20s and 30s, but I even older folks, too—some of them are parents of the kids who watched the show. So now we relive fun things I did on the show, and I still share little funny jokes and contests and goofy video challenges. I get a chance to hear all their stories about watching and being in the show and it brings it all back to me.

A lot of my viewers were latchkey kids who told me later as adults that my show was one of the only bright spots in their days. They leave notes on my Facebook page telling me that I helped them to find some laughter every day, and that I kind of saved their life. That means a lot to me, even now, knowing that all my hard work did make a difference in those kids' lives…it gives me enormous joy.

It's because of my Facebook fans that this whole book project began. I've had hundreds and hundreds of people ask me for some way to interact even more deeply now as adults. So if you happen to be one of those people, I hope this brings you a lot of fun. My big wish is to zip maximum joy into your life and to remind you that you can lead a Big Happy Life every day of the year."

☺ There is no greater joy nor greater reward than to make a fundamental difference in someone's life.

> **"If you choose goals that fit your lifestyle and strengths, you'll be more likely to persist at them and achieve them —and that will make you happier." ~ Sonja Lyubomirsky**

Look back over your own shoulder

Is there anything in your past that you might like to revisit in the internet age? Do you have accomplishments you might want to build on? The ease of connecting online with new people and reconnecting with old friends is downright magical—how could you put that to use to find new forms of happiness? What would you regret never trying?

People regret *not doing things* more than they regret the things they did, even if what they did wasn't all that great. Mike has no regrets; he has gone all out for everything he ever wanted. Not getting some of them is fine…sometimes it's for the better. **Here's a little secret:** as recently as 2012 Mike prepared a proposal for a NEW TV show at the request of a well-known production company. For a few weeks he was quite excited by the prospect. When it turned out that the timing wasn't right on their end, it suddenly became clear it wasn't right on Mike's end, either.

☺Be willing to embrace the unknown. You don't have to know the whole route between here and there, just take the first step now toward Your Big Happy Life.

Here's a really BIG ta da moment (sound the trumpets!)
In this chapter we've served up a fine buffet of ideas and methods for envisioning your own Big Happy Life. Once you're clear how you want that to look, **it's time to make a binding commitment to yourself** to bring it to fruition. (Isn't that a fun word? It ought to taste like grapes and berries. But we digress.) To make it real, you can write out your own promise certificate / contract / poster to sign and keep. For maximum benefit, hang it in a prominent place. We like the idea of a contract, because once it's signed, it becomes legal and binding, a contract between the Current You and the Future You. In it you agree to do whatever it takes to provide a bigger, happier life for yourself. Besides, studies say the act of signing it increases your happiness, because it imparts a sense of control over your life…and maybe some smug satisfaction that you're doing a good thing. As a bonus, research shows that making an oath to perform a behavior increases the likelihood that action will be taken.

Once you start something, the only path to joy is to finish it. Shout it out: **I WILL do this! I have a vision for my Big Happy Life, and I commit to making it real. I take responsibility for how my life unfolds, and I hold the power gleefully.**

"You create your opportunities by asking for them."
~Shakti Gawain

> "I don't want to get to the end of my life and find that I lived just the length of it. I want to have lived the width of it as well."
> ~Diane Ackerman

AFFIRMATIONS: I am already living my Big Happy Life and it is amazing! I infuse every aspect of my life with more awareness, deeper meaning and absolute joy in all I do. I make good choices about how I use my time and that brings happiness, too. I enjoy expressing myself above and beyond what I thought I could do—my true potential is limitless.

> "I believe that when you realize who you really are, you understand that nothing can stop you from becoming that person."
> ~ Christine Lincoln

> "Our aspirations are our possibilities." ~ Samuel Johnson

In the next chapter: Can you guess what comes next? Betcha can. Here's a hint: *mplmnttn*. Would you like to buy a vowel? Vanna, give the viewer an "i"…now you've got it.

Chapter Five
Create Your Big Happy Life
   attaining your vision

In this chapter:
- ✓ Ideas are meant to be revised
- ✓ The evolution of your dream
- ✓ Making it bigger
- ✓ Making it real
- ✓ How to affirm for impact
- ✓ Peek into the future
- ✓ Get going now
- ✓ Every single day, yes!
- ✓ Mundane no longer exists
- ✓ Emotional house cleaning
- ✓ You're more creative than you think
- ✓ It's not a rock
- ✓ Take another look
- ✓ Applause on demand
- ✓ Does this add to your joy?

> **"Never fear the space between your dreams and your reality. If you can dream it, you can make it so."** ~Belva Davis

Just do it!

If you've been playing along with the home game, by now you have some sort of vision of how you'd like Your Big Happy Life to look and feel. Sweet! Now it's time to drag those dreams out of your head (it won't hurt) and breathe life into them. As preparation for this endeavor, we've given you many fun ways to extract more day out of your days (Chapter Two). We've shown you how to experience joy to the fullest extent your personal laws will allow (Chapter Three). And we've lit a passionate fire in your heart to live a fuller life (Chapter Four). In this chapter we bring all those steps together, but first Mike would like to inspire you with more of his story. (This is the tasty part!)

On his epic list of 167 life goals that he felt would bring him joy, Mike finally got around to #112: Invent and market a product. It happened one day back in the 20th century at his favorite Chinese restaurant. When the same old boring fortune cookies arrived at the table, that's when Mike had his light bulb moment, when he *knew* he had his BIG idea. The cookies were dull looking, bland in flavor and usually had dumb fortunes in them (*You will buy new clothes*). Duh! It was like eating cardboard, and the fortunes were always printed on flimsy paper that ripped easily—all things Mike figured he could improve upon.

> **"If a window of opportunity appears, don't pull down the shade."**
> ~Tom Peters

IN (AND OUT) OF MIKE'S MOUTH:

"Sitting there my excitement level went through the roof, because I was sure I just had a million dollar idea. *Tada!* I invented Fancy Fortune Cookies, the very first flavored, colored, gourmet fortune cookies. I'm sure I was inspired by all those years of playing a clown in bright colors.

It required a lot of hard work to manifest my dream, and I didn't have much support. All my friends and family thought I was out of my mind. They just didn't believe other people would get excited by a new kind of fortune cookie. I heard that hundreds and hundreds of times, but I just leapt into the vat of dough. (Not really, but things were pretty sticky at the start.) It was exciting to pursue my vision, even though I had NO manufacturing experience whatsoever, but I didn't let that stop me. I went from businessman to businessman asking for advice and help, and every time I shared my idea **I kept getting the same reaction—that I was nuts just because I wanted to do something fun and new**. Finally I found someone to help me develop my colors and flavors, even though he didn't really get it either.

I started with three colors and I called them Fortune Kookies for Kids, which evolved from watching the kids in my audience at *Happy's Place*. When they came to the show we always gave them candy, and there was something so joyful about watching a big bunch of kids get excited by (and truth be told, hopped up on!) surprise candy. My first three flavors were orange, green mint and strawberry. It took us three years to develop twelve flavors. Today we bake 25 flavors and 29 colors, but it took many years to reach those numbers.

In the early years **I knew I had to champion my own ideas since no one else was coming forward with applause back then.**

It's been almost 25 years since I first invented gourmet fortune cookies. Eventually, my hard work paid off, and one of the signs of success was other cookie bakers trying to mimic my products. As the pioneer, I'm the one out in front with a lot of arrows in my back. I have about 9,000 punctures in my hide from all the arrows shot at me by competitors and copycats. Over the years we continued to innovate, adding three flavors of chocolate dipping, then caramel. We offer personalized fortunes and print them on durable paper for everyone who likes to save them. And because we also sprinkle our dipped cookies with colorful candy, crushed nuts and even ginger snaps, there are nearly endless combinations we can bake.

Continuing to innovate and monkey around with fortune cookies is what keeps me jazzed and happy to still be in this business so many years later. To this day I still ask: What else can I do differently? I want to stay waaay ahead of my competition. It helps that I know what my vision is. What I've always said is: I don't bake cookies —I sell smiles—I think of myself as being in the joy business."

"The secret of getting ahead is getting started." ~Sally Berger

☺Joy is the beginning of the journey, its end, and the journey itself.

"Even if it meant being crazy and out of step with all that seemed holy, I had decided to be me." ~M. Scott Peck

Though Mike had plenty of naysayers around him (and we'll put them in their place in the next chapter) he still managed to manifest his Big Happy Life. One way he did it was to stay in motion, always looking for ways to improve his business and his life. **He never stopped learning and experimenting; he never stopped, period.**

"What is not started today is never finished tomorrow." ~Goethe

MIKE'S STILL TALKING
(AND WEARING HIS MAD SCIENTIST WIG):
"I love the mental gymnastics of inventing, of taking a good idea and making it superior, of taking a solid, marketable concept and pushing it even farther and wilder. Even though I set aside my clown personas for awhile, it was the playfulness and inventiveness of clowning that made me a good inventor. You can do the same with your own ideas, with your vision of Your Big Happy Life. **As you begin to implement your ideas, always be ready to revise, enhance, improve and expand your**

original thoughts, which is where the fun lies, because it's okay that your plans are always evolving. It's not that this vision is a fixed blueprint for the life your building, it's really about getting you to open to greater possibilities, to get you dreaming and imagining a bigger, happier life."

"Everyone who has ever taken a shower has had an idea. It's the person who gets out of the shower, dries off, and does something about it who makes a difference."
~Nolan Bushnell

How might your vision evolve? Were there other ideas you had while reading the last chapter that you discarded as being too far out, too difficult or improbable? Rescue them from the wastebasket! **Nag alert:** we really, truly, deeply pray that you're journaling or keeping some sort of notebook about this process, because that's a perfect place to tuck away your craziest ideas. You never know when one of those may spark a variation that you do decide to animate. If you've never thought of yourself as an innovator or an entrepreneur, we challenge you to try on that hat for awhile—we're certain you'd look fetching. It really does help to look at ideas from weird angles, even from the vantage point of imagining your life as a product. How would you manufacture your Big Happy Life? What does your packaging look like? What's new and improved?

"Planning is bringing the future into the present so that you can do something about it now." ~Alan Lakein

☺**We double dog dare you:** Try taking a concrete step today toward one of your goals (it doesn't matter which one) **BUT try and do it differently** than you'd ordinarily think of doing it. The operative word being *ordinarily*. We believe we've already established that you have little interest in leading an ordinary life. Do it with panache, with flash, with flair!

"Don't wait for your ship to come in and feel angry and cheated when it doesn't. Get going with something small." ~Irene Kassorla

MORE MIKE:
"With my fortune cookie company, one of my innovations was to think about my cookies in a much BIGGER way. So I invented the world's largest fortune cookie…our giants weigh over one pound. The fortune is over a foot long and we print it in full color—*bigger, bigger, bigger*. Now we bake them in colors and flavors, too. We even invented special equipment to make these gigandos. **If you stare at your life and your vision for it long enough, new ideas may emerge.** Ask yourself: What would inventor extraordinaire Ben Franklin do? That's when the magic really happens…when you hit on a new aspect of your vision, then other ways of applying it multiply like, well, rabbits. (Or good happits!)"

Happit: *enlarging* Just when you thought you were done creating you own vision, we challenge you to dream even BIGGER, to open up to the full rainbow of possibilities for Your Big Happy Life. Take every idea you have, no matter how tiny, examine it and find a way to make it even a little bit bigger—and when you can, make it a LOT bigger. (And bigger doesn't have to mean literally larger in size. Think regional not local; global not national; a deeper meaning, a greater value.) **Every day for the next 21 days find at least one way to expand your vision for Your Big Happy Life.** Imagine how much richer it will become in just three short weeks! A life is only as big as the dream you dare to live.

**"Nearly everyone takes the limits of his own vision for the limits of the world. A few do not. Join them."
~Arthur Schopenhauer**

"Start by doing what is necessary, then what is possible, and suddenly you are doing the impossible."
~St. Francis of Assisi

MIKE CONTINUES:
"You can't be afraid to monkey around with your Big Happy Life. Play with all aspects of your ideas, turn them upside down and inside out… colorize them…your life doesn't have to resemble anyone else's life. You can be as wild and crazy in living your life as you want to be. Make a mind map of your life, and include some new destinations on it. Go bananas—move to Ecuador, where bananas grow wild. Set an intention to dream about your new life at night—and remember it! Especially if you aren't in love with how you now spend most of your time, reinvention is a must. What did you want to be when you grew up? What happened? Maybe it's not too late."

"A mind stretched by a new idea can never go back to its original dimension." ~Oliver Wendell Holmes

Sustain your vision and don't lose sight of it
If you don't keep your vision centrally located in your consciousness as you begin creating Your Big Happy Life, it will probably fade away into the background of your human doingness. Finishing that report will take precedence over reading that grad school catalog, which isn't so bad. But then you discover that hanging out with your pals and yammering about your messed up lives supersedes doing something about it. If you're not careful, all the sparkly ideas you dreamed up while reading this book will vanish into the fog of creeping boredom or depression that you poked your head temporarily out of.

To combat that grim scenario, surround yourself with messages that reinforce your dreams. **We love affirmations—but the secret is to supercharge them**, to make them not just a mental practice but a physical one. Don't forget, you may know what you want, but you get what you expect.

> **"Here in this moment, imagine you have everything.
> That will begin to give you an inkling of who you are."
> ~Marianne Williamson**

Happit: *affirming* You've undoubtedly heard the affirmation spiel before (and perhaps you've tried a version that didn't work for you). That's because **repeating intentions only helps if it inspires you to take ACTION on your desires**. That said, you *can* infuse your affirmation practice with extra oomph if you combine it with physicality, such as: saying—or shouting—them aloud; walking or running while you say them; do them to music and dance; say several sets of them while on a treadmill or bike. Mike does jumping jacks or cartwheels while shouting affirmations. Oriana says them aloud to Vivaldi every morning. **Write out a flock of affirmations using present tense, stating what you want as though you already have it.** Repeat them daily for—you guessed it—21 days straight (or curved) (or zigged) (or zagged). Examples:
- ♣ NOT: I'll be happy if I get a job at NASA. INSTEAD: I am happily employed as a Martian cartographer.
- ♣ NOT: I avoid all foods that are bad for me. INSTEAD: I am healthier than I've ever been, and I savor eating food that enhances my great health.
- ♣ NOT: I stop being depressed because I'm still single. INSTEAD: I love being in a nurturing relationship with a caring, sensitive partner.
- ♣ NOT: I no longer need to work 18-hour days. INSTEAD: I value my personal time, and I create a healthy balance between work and pleasure.

♣ NOT: I break my habit of obsessing all over eBay for vintage troll dolls. INSTEAD: I enjoy my troll collection and believe I have more than enough to enjoy them in every room of my house.

"You can have anything you want if you are willing to give up the belief that you can't have it." ~Robert Anthony

**"I know for sure that what we dwell on is who we become."
~ Oprah Winfrey**

Enter the third dimension

Next, take your vision up a few notches by creating 3-D representations of Your Big Happy Life, as well as some motivational objects. Make them as lively, colorful and wacktastic as possible. Options include:
- ✦ **treasure maps** or dream maps with 3-D objects
- ✦ a video or **screensaver** for your computer that represents your new reality and reinforces your goals
- ✦ a good old fashioned collage of what you want and where you are going
- ✦ **record yourself doing your affirmations**, then load it into your MP3 player or burn a CD if you're old school
- ✦ make a **tiny vignette or display** that represents what you want your life to look like; place it right below your desktop monitor or anywhere you'll see it daily
- ✦ make or buy some **jewelry** that symbolizes your goals and wear it often (a charm bracelet or necklace is great for this)
- ✦ have your core values **tattooed** somewhere you can see them easily
- ✦ fold a copy of your vision or your Joy List into an **origami** sculpture
- ✦ **print your affirmations** on a T-shirt for your dog, then you can read them aloud while you go for your rambles

> **"If what's in your dreams wasn't already real inside you, you couldn't even dream it." ~Gloria Steinem**

☺ Live your Big Happy Life in Technicolor

How vivid is your life? Look around…what do you see? Do you need more color in your life? Neutrals are so nowhere. Neutrals say: I don't know who I am, or I'm afraid to tell the world what I like. Spatulas come in pink, paper clips in purple. Go buy some red shoes. Turquoise underwear. Chartreuse sheets. Play with polka dots. Fuchsia is the new black. Focus magnifies whatever is there…on what do you dwell?

> **"What we can or cannot do, what we consider possible or impossible, is rarely a function of our true capability.
> It is more likely a function of our beliefs about who we are."
> ~Anthony Robbins**

Enjoy your virtual reality

Mike suspects that you've probably wasted many perfectly good hours on Pinterest. Perhaps you spend a wee bit too much time wishing instead of doing. As of this writing, Pinterest is already the #3 social website on earth! Want to know why? Because our brains CANNOT distinguish between images we look at and the real thing, so grazing on Pinterest is like really BEING there. We get the same endorphin rush that we'd get if we could attend the glamorous wedding, lounge on the tropical beach, relax in the glorious garden. Of course it's not really as good, but we do get a chemical buzz from all the eye candy.

So how can you put the phenomenon to work in service of actually *attaining* your dreams? You can make your own Pinterest boards (it's free) that create a facsimile of the life you're working toward, a sort of preview of what you intend to manifest in the real world. The value of it is that whenever your energy wanes or your enthusiasm implodes, you can zip it back up with a virtual trip to Your

Big Happy Life. CAUTION: just don't fall into the trap of *only* enjoying your virtual life—**it's a tool to get you to make it real.**

Happit: *previewing* For 21 days in a row, add new items to your Pinterest boards that represent Your Big Happy Life. **See how much emotion you can stir up and attach to them, which is a key to their effectiveness.**
Believe in your dreams and they may come true; believe in yourself and they will come true.

> "Only I can change my life. No one can do it for me."
> ~Carol Burnett

☺ The positive thinker sees the invisible, feels the intangible, and achieves the impossible. (And it's impossible to be angry while looking at a penguin. Try it.)

> "What you can do, or dream you can do, begin it;
> boldness has genius, power and magic in it." ~Goethe

And here's a BIG secret. **As much as we want you to visualize your own Big Happy Life—and it IS a key step—the point isn't your vision or the goals you set to reach it.**
- ✳ It's about *pursuing* your dreams and how that shapes your life in unexpected and marvelous ways into something else entirely.
- ✳ It's about *going after* those goals and how that adds dimension and purpose to your life, plus a lot more fun along the way.
- ✳ It's about *gaining clarity* on your values and how that provides meaning and fulfillment to your journey.

The Founding Fathers understood that ***the pursuit of happiness*** is happy-making itself. Remember all those games of monopoly you played as a kid? Was the fun in the five seconds of gloating when you won, or was it in the three hours it took to play the game? If it was only about winning, ESPN could just show the last 60 seconds of every game (much to many wives' delight). No, the real joy is experienced all along the way as you test yourself, overcome challenges and revel in your growth. Of course, it's rewarding to reach some of your goals, but **reaching them is not the *source* of happiness. Setting off after them in the first place is when the happy hops in.**

"Steering your boat down the river of time is a source of pleasure, regardless of your ports of call." ~Someone WhoLivedFully

The whole point of Chapter Four was to get you to envision the kind of life you want, and the point of this chapter is to inspire you to start moving toward those dreams. It's the moving that revs up the joy machine in your soul. (It's in there, trust us.) If you cannot find happiness along the road, you will not find it at the end of the road.

"Live your life each day as you would climb a mountain. An occasional glance towards the summit keeps the goal in mind, but many beautiful scenes are to be observed from each new vantage point." ~Harold B. Melchart

"Far away there in the sunshine are my highest aspirations. I may not reach them, but I can look up and see their beauty, believe in them, and try to follow where they lead." ~Louisa May Alcott

Do it every single day no matter what, Nyquil or no Nyquil

It ought to be obvious (and it may be to some people) but if you never take action on your vision, it will remain, well, this floaty gossamer entity that flits around your mind now and then, growing ever more faint as it withers from lack of energy applied to it. We want you to be a dreamer—but also a doer—yes even on days when you're home with a cold. (Now THAT'S a good time to play on Pinterest!) Don't let yourself get trapped in perfecting your vision. **Remember, the point of**

the vision is to inspire you to take action. And don't makes excuses not to start. No one will grade you. Just take one eensy teensy step in private. Go on, we'll wait. Really, do it right now.

Well? That wasn't so hard, was it? Told you so!

Two words: finish stuff.
Two more: stop procrastinating.
Bonus duo: right now.

Happit: *continuing* If you have a big project or goal you want to work toward as part of Your Big Happy Life, challenge yourself to put in some daily effort for each of those magical 21 days. Promise to devote 15 minutes minimally, as they are the toughest. After the first 15 minutes, you may well keep going and shock yourself how much you can do at oh:dark:thirty. After three weeks you'll be happitized to complete your project…and won't that feel good! To help you with this, you might make a **nag sign** for your mirror that not-so-gently nudges you to do one thing daily.

> "You don't have to be great to get started, but you do have to get started to be great." ~Les Brown

MORE FROM MIKE:
"It's a Law of Physics…if you take steps every single day toward Your Big Happy Life you WILL get there! I guarantee it. Whether you're trying to change your mindset, makeover your body, or edit your relationships, it makes no difference. **Keep moving toward your vision and it will come to life.** Constant progress is the name of this game (and do remember to keep it fun). Say it with me: *Today I'm going to have more fun than yesterday, and tomorrow I'm going to have more fun than today!* Besides, daily action creates momentum, which accelerates your

progress. Before you know it, you're zooming along manifesting your new life today. **Today! Not tomorrow, today!"**

Happit: *beginning* It's time to get doing (that's not a typo). **On Day One make a list of OVER 21 new ways you could add joy to your life**, then do one of them every day for 21 days. Why more than 21? Cuz some will be duds! If one tanks, pick another one, then you don't have an excuse to give up before you're done. (Some of you give up too easily, and we know who you are!) Whether you think you're ready or not, just start right now. There is magic in action.

**"Every day I make an effort to go toward what I don't understand."
~Yo-Yo Ma**

Face Your Big Happy Life
If you keep your dreams inside your head they're much harder to manifest. **Do whatever it takes to keep your vision in front of your face:**
- write it on the walls
- frame your affirmations
- stick reminders in your wallet
- use post-it notes and put them all over the house
- write it on a mirror so you can contemplate it several times a day
- Mike even posts small notes on the side window of his car!

Print your values, key truths, Joy List and anything pertinent in a huge font and tape them to your walls. For a long time Mike had this emblazoned on his office wall: *If it ain't fun, I ain't doing it!* So when someone would call him and ask him to do something, he'd glance at that sign and immediately know whether or not it was something he wanted to do. Whatever your particular challenge is, focus on that.

Happit: *funning* We're both big list makers, and as with every other tip in this book, there are ways to do it with more joy. Use colored or patterned paper, bright pens, collaged images for inspiration—whatever will make you take notice (and action) when you see your list. Oriana has a guilty pleasure collecting stickers, which stems from her decade of piano lessons as a kid. Her teacher stuck a snazzy sticker on each piece of music she learned, which was brilliant motivation for a budding artist. Now she literally gives herself gold stars for Big Time Accomplishments. What would make it fun for you? **For those magical 21 days do some mundane thing in a radically big fun way.**

- Hauling the recycling to the curb? Rescue an item and upcycle it into something useful.
- Giving your dog a bath? Tint her pink with food coloring (doesn't work so well on black dogs!).
- Taking your car in for an oil change? Bring donuts for the crew (extreme ones with chocolate and sprinkles).
- Reviewing your fourth grader's book report? Help her illustrate it in living color. Or make a power point presentation about it. Or a music video.

Every single dull chore you do all day long CAN be made more fun. Do it for 21 days in a row and you'll do it forever. Now THAT'S a Big Happy Life!

"There are no shortcuts to any place worth going."
~Beverly Sills

MORE FROM MIKE:
"One of the keys to implementing significant life changes is learning how to **juggle** aspects of your life in such a way that you **ALWAYS make time** to **pursue your dreams**—working toward your vision **NEVER** gets put on a back burner or a closet shelf."

"How does one become a butterfly? You must want to fly so much that you're willing to give up being a caterpillar." ~Trina Paulus

How happy are you today?
Remember way back in Chapter One we introduced our Joy Scale and showed you how to find your **Happy Number**? So have you been using it? If not, now would be a good time to start as you forge ahead into creation mode. If your number today is more contrary than merry, then use that number as impetus to take action. Just until it shifts, you might chart your number hour by hour and see if you can ease it up the meter. Don't get too comfy in the middle range of the Joy Scale… remind yourself of what you want and stay motivated to put more energy into attaining your vision. **So ironically, the *lower* your Happy Number is right now, the easier it will be for you to use it to inspire your forward movement.**

☺ **Even if every day may not be good, there is always something good in every day.** (Some days you may have to look for it with more diligence…even get down on the floor and search under the bed…hey, get rid of those dust bunnies while you're at it.)

For maximum happiness...be careful of comfort; instead, stretch and extend yourself regularly. **The more of an irritant your present reality is, the more likely you are to push ahead for change.** That's why so many people stop just *before* they reach their goal—because they've reached some version of it, and their irritant has been soothed. They do make progress, their life is getting better, but they don't stretch themselves for that last mile to really reach their ultimate goal.

Happit: *enduring* Stay in intimate contact with your irritant for 21 days and find creative ways to let it inspire your forward progress. For example, if your goal is to buy your first house and the irritant is living in cramped quarters surrounded by noisy neighbors, then really take that in. Note in your journal all the daily annoyances you endure. If your upstairs neighbor lifts clunky weights at 6 a.m., take out your earplugs and count how many times he drops his barbell on the floor above your bed. Use your anger to do whatever it takes to save the money to get the hell out of that Dodge. **If you just avoid or squelch your irritants, they can't help you.**

> "Don't be afraid of shadows, they just mean there's a light shining somewhere near." ~Bright Thinker

MIKE CONFIDES:

"**Psst….here's another secret:** While you'd like to have a pleasant day every day, it doesn't matter as much how happy you are on any *one* day, it's far more important how your life is *evolving*. In other words, **it matters that as each year goes by, you GET HAPPIER because you're implementing more activities and practices that add joy to your life. You're reaching some of your goals, taking more responsibility for your happiness and leading a more fulfilled life**. The worst thing you can do is to put them all on hold, thinking: "Oh I have plenty of time to climb that mountain…I'm only 30 or 39 or 45…" Why on earth would you want to *delay* more happiness? Good answer! How cool is it that you don't need to wait a single second to start improving your life!"

> "Greatness is not in where we stand, but what direction we are moving. We must sail sometimes with the wind and, sometimes against. But sail we must and not drift nor lie at anchor."
> ~ **Oliver Wendell Holmes**

> "Your life can explode with potential that had little possibility of developing the day before, if you are open to it." ~**Gary Zukav**

We're taking the broom out for a spin
No, it's not Halloween, but it might be scary. Please consider this: Happiness is both what you *have* in your life and what you *don't have*. (And we're talking **in**tangibles here, not Cuisinart immersion blenders or HD 3D wondervision.) It's an old truism that cleaning your physical space and emptying your closets makes room for better things in your life. Well, so does emotional house cleaning. What? You've never manned an imaginary swiffer? We'll show you how.

Start by making a list of all the intangible things that weigh you down and clutter your life, such as:
* **Obligations you don't really want.** (Museum docent? Who were you trying to impress? Your Mother-in-law?)
* **Other people's dreams for you.** (You're never going to join your Dad's firm, so man up and tell him so.)
* **Half-baked goals lined up like a gauntlet of taunting teens.** (That's what filing cabinets and Carbonite subscriptions are for.)
* **Strict rules you feel you ought to abide.** (Unless we're talking legalities or the Uniform Building Code, then whether you follow someone else's ideas is your call.)
* **Compulsive ideas about actual house cleaning.** (No one ever died of shame because some dust accumulated on their étagère.) Our kind of house cleaning is better for your soul.

The upshot of making this Weighty List, is you can decide what no longer serves you in pursuit of Your Big Happy Life and flush that stuff down the virtual youknowwhat. Which in turn creates more space in your head and heart for things that really matter. (And if you've been reading these chapters in order, you figured out what *those* are in Chapter Four.)

☺**Order from chaos frees up energy.** Back on the physical plane, organizing your actual living and working spaces does create an inner calm for most people. It's a way of quieting visual noise, of enabling focus. Learn to love color-coded file folders, designer three-ring binders and alphabetical soups. (Well, maybe not that last one, but you get the idea.) Also look for things that inspire negative thoughts and give them the heave-ho—framed photos of naysayers, gifts you never liked from people you didn't feel so good about either, and so on.

Who do you look up to?

If you're lacking in motivation to get started on something it can help to absorb some wisdom from someone you admire. That's one reason we've included so many inspirational quotes from such diverse sources, so that some of them are sure to appeal to you and give you a boost when you need one. But you can be more focused about it, too. Oriana likes to fire up some TED Talks on YouTube, and Mike loves reading biographies of successful people and seeing what obstacles they overcame on their journeys. **Knowing what you admire in other people can be a reflection of your own aspirations.**

MIKE'S KICKASS MEMORY:
"I was lucky because at a young age—12 and 13—I idolized someone famous who lead me to thinking more deeply about life, how to improve my life and how I could become the best possible person in every aspect of my life. My idol was the world's biggest box office star—Bruce Lee. Everything he did I watched. I practiced for hours in the mirror to try and become like him. I studied martial arts, which also started me on a path of developing my physical skills. I read everything written about him. He epitomized someone who can improve and grow every day. He taught me **that it's possible to expand the amount of happiness you have in your life every single day.**"

☺ **Who can you model some aspects of your life on?** Be prepared for times of low mojo and have some inspirational materials on hand, then you don't have to let a whole day waft by on a polluted contrail of downward droopiness.

> **"It takes a lot of courage to release the familiar and seemingly secure, to embrace the new. But there is no real security in what is no longer meaningful. There is more security in the adventurous and exciting, for in movement there is life, and in change there is power and joy."** ~Alan Cohen

☺ **What's new Pussycat?** Consider the power of **novelty** to add more springiness to your life. When's the last time you tried a new food? Ever eaten rambutan or physalis? Life's too short to limit your options to apples and oranges. Dance with a star (we hear Arcturus does a killer rumba). Swim with a manatee.
Shop for enchanting headgear in China.

Creativity is an aspect of happiness

Yes, Virginia, everyone really is an artist in their own way...can't draw a straight line? That's what rulers are for. Add some form of creativity to your life: cooking and developing new recipes, scrapbooking, gardening, knitting, upholstery, furniture refinishing, home decorating—there's a reason those are called *domestic arts*—because the old-fashioned notion of keeping a beautiful, nurturing home is absolutely an art form. Sadly, in our rushed society, home keeping often devolves into a list of chores suitable only for family browbeating festivals.

The self-satisfaction that arises when you create something with your own two hands (like someone else would lend you theirs!) is impossible to overstate. If you never thought of yourself as the artsy craftsy type, you owe it to yourself to try anyway. **Even the most modest achievements can jazz up your joy levels.** Now with the ever-present internet, you can learn to do just about anything you can imagine—and 10,982 things you haven't. Pick one. And start. Today.

"If you want to draw, you must shut your eyes and sing."
~Pablo Picasso

MIKE BLISSES OUT:
"Having fun is a way to spark creativity. Instead of doing things the way everyone else does, try doing the exact opposite—and that's a route to both joy and success. Pushing outside boundaries stretches your brain, creates new pathways for original thinking. Infusing your life with more fun juices it up, jacks it up to a whole new level, and that allows you to be even *more* creative in your thinking. Part of living a Big Happy Life is to be as creative as you possibly can in all your thinking."

"There is a fountain of youth: it is your mind, your talents, the creativity you bring to your life and the lives of the people you love. When you learn to tap this source, you will truly have defeated age."
~Sophia Loren

There will be flops, but they don't have to drop you
MIKE ROLLS ON THE FLOOR LAUGHING:
"Taking my own advice, I went even wilder and pushed myself to develop fortune cookie flavors no one else had ever considered, like bubble gum and cotton candy, which are still in our line. I tried the hazelnut liqueur Frangelico, then cappuccino, which is a bestseller and my best smeller. But I also had lots of scary flops! We even made a hot pepper oregano, which nearly killed us, because it polluted the whole bakery while we were experimenting with it. Then came the biggest fail…what was I thinking…pepperoni fortune cookies? **That was the worst tasting flavor in fortune cookie history!** (I didn't fall. I attacked the floor.) But all along the experimental highway we continued to have

fun. Life always provides both hits and misses, but that makes it exciting, which is part of living a big life. **Take some risks!"**

**"Forget past mistakes. Forget failures. Forget everything except what you're going to do now and do it."
~William Durant, founder of General Motors**

"You may be disappointed if you fail, but you are doomed if you don't try." ~Beverly Sills

**"Success is not the key to happiness. Happiness is the key to success. If you love what you're doing, you will be successful."
~Albert Schweitzer**

"Do not follow where the path may lead. Go instead where there is no path and leave a trail." ~Muriel Strode

The road to your Big Happy Life is NOT called Easy Street
There will be rocks and potholes in your road. Your plans will go awry. Your vision will contain ideas that get rejected, but you can choose to view that as a challenge to overcome—*creatively*. We are all faced with a series of great opportunities brilliantly disguised as impossible situations. It's difficult to follow your dream, but it's a tragedy not to. Think so far outside the box that you can't remember what walls even look like.

- ❖ Perhaps you apply for a grant or a scholarship and don't get it. What other avenues can you take? These days you can get a degree online in almost anything at a fraction of the cost of traditional college.
- ❖ Maybe you start a brew-beer-at-home business without having enough capital and it goes beer belly up. What can you learn from that—besides being better funded? Do more research, crowd

source some feedback online and see if you can't retool and resurrect your business in a better form. Investigate micro-funding.
- ❖ Suppose you're eager to settle down, but all your dating adventures end in heartbreak or restraining orders. Do you have to give up? No way! Invest in a professional matchmaker, which may produce much better results than desperate4love.me . Have a Facebook contest to find you a mate. Leave tantalizing tidbits about yourself in geo-caches. Pursue so many crazy stunts and oddball schemes to find love that you become newsworthy and get on *Good Morning Memphis*, and that becomes your cute meet. (A romance writer's term for how a love match begins.)

"Our doubts are traitors and make us lose the good we often might win, by fearing to attempt our dreams." ~Jane Addams

"Being defeated is often a temporary condition. Giving up is what makes it permanent." ~Marilyn vos Savant

Set back to move forward
Besides his flavor fails, Mike had some monumental setbacks in his business life—some that might have shut down another man's dreams. But not Mike. Nosiree Bob. (Who's Bob?)

MIKE BOUNCES BACK:
"Setbacks are inevitable, and I've had my share, starting with having all my money embezzled. I woke up one morning with $5.63 in my pocket! Going to the bank and finding that out was certainly dramatic. I've also had my ideas stolen along the way. Sometimes you have to take legal action, which is never fun, but there's always something to be learned from it."

When setbacks occur, honestly analyze your situation:
- Why did this happen?
- What are the bare facts of the situation?
- Did you do something wrong?

- Did you take on the wrong partner?
- Did you fail to do enough research?
- Or did you just ask the wrong people?
- What could you have done differently?
- Was your idea flawed in some way?
- Do you need to learn a new skill?
- What can be salvaged from this setback?
- Was the egg salad past its expiration date?

There's always an insight to be gained. Then when the next setback occurs, you'll be more nimble, more self-confident and better able to respond.

"You're never a loser until you quit trying." ~Mike Ditka

☺ News flash! Money CAN buy happiness in some situations. How? Spending money on things that make your work life easier, that end frustration, that create flow, can indeed cause more happiness.

"The most successful people are those who are good at Plan B." ~James Yorke

Into every life a little rain must fall

Despite being an extraordinary purveyor or Happiness, Mike still has an occasional day when his high spirits hit a low point. If it were not for dark clouds, we wouldn't know how to appreciate the sunshine. It's human nature for our moods to ebb and flow, but Mike believes you can push the tide toward more flow and less ebb. (Don't send us letters about tidal geography, please.) **No one can be honestly happy all the time and that's okay.** (Well maybe the transcended among us can, but they're hiding out in high elevation huts.)

The rest of us mortals need to face reality when we experience a day or so of blank blahs. Especially after an intensely joyful period, it's inevitable that by contrast the following days will be paler. **The key is**

not to see that as failure. We need lesser days in order to appreciate greater ones. There's a rhythm to life and the soundtrack isn't always playing your song. (What's yours? Mike's is—what else?—*Don't Worry Be Happy*.) **Look at your down days as down time**—an opportunity to regroup and prepare for a new cycle of growth. Without that irritating pebble in its midst, the oyster cannot birth a pearl.

> "The way I see it, if you want the rainbow,
> you gotta put up with the rain." ~Dolly Parton

> "Life isn't about waiting for the storm to pass...
> it's about learning to dance in the rain." ~Vivian Greene

Do you see a boulder or a stepping stone?
Two people, same rock, different response. What's yours? How you react to (perceived) adversity can make a world of difference. **There's a golden moment in time between what happens to you and how you react to it.** What you do in that moment holds another key to happiness: the ability to *choose* your response.

Once upon a time Oriana was suddenly let go from a job she loved after many years with the company. After rebounding from the initial shock, she set about to find the gift in her unsettling situation. Within 24 hours she called her boss to thank him for releasing her to live a much larger version of her life. She'd become so cozy and comfortable in her position that she'd forgotten some of her dreams, and she was grateful to make a course correction.

Can you think of a time when life hit you on the head with a cosmic bat and you didn't see it coming? How did you handle it? Some people like to attend their own pity parties and collect condolences for their crappy luck. And others prefer anchovies to chocolate, but there's no accounting for some people's taste. Us, we'd rather step back, examine the situation carefully and look for the lesson, the gift in the event. It's always there. Every time. Even the most tragic circumstances can spawn foundations and movements that change the world. Think of all the Mothers Against Drunk Driving. Of course they grieved. But they also got mad and they got MADD.

> **"I'm not afraid of storms, for I'm learning to sail my ship."**
> **~Louisa May Alcott**

Happit: *spinning* **Every day for the next 21 days look for something negative to turn upside down.** (Even if some days you have to borrow someone else's sadness.) This is mostly a mental exercise, though it could also lead you to take action. **It can be trivial:** You break the heel off your ruby red pumps. *They hurt your feet because you bought them a half size too small, so good riddance!* **Or it may be a bigger deal:** You learn your brother needs a bone marrow transplant. *Which gives you a chance to step up and see if you're a match, which repairs an old rift between you.* It might only take a few seconds some days, or it may take an hour of soul searching on another. **The point is to not give up until you find the pearl…which is yours to keep.** You're welcome.

    And therein lies the secret to life: No matter what happens in your life, the *meaning* of what has happened is yours. Life is 10% circumstance and 90% your response.

> **"Life is like a camera. Just focus on what's important**
> **and capture the good times, develop from the negatives,**
> **or just take another shot." ~Ansel Sureshot**

Failure? Forgedaboudit!
    Many people fear failure (and surprisingly some fear success). One reason some people slip into depression is **an instinct we have to remember our failures**, and along with them the consequences of our failing. In an evolutionary sense, if you barely moved fast enough to outrun the saber-toothed tiger hot on your trail, then having a vivid memory of your near-miss is a teachable moment. These days most of

the monsters chasing you are of your own creation. Today it makes no sense to fear taking action because you falsely believe failure is inevitable. If you do that, you're expecting defeat before it even happens—and affirming it will happen, too.

Conversely, some people sabotage their success because of what the consequences might be. They fear earning more than their parents, outshining a partner, attaining fame, the added pressures of promotions—and on and on and on. That's why Mike stressed clarity so much in the last chapter—if you know what level of success you want, then it's a whole lot easier to get there (and enjoy it when you arrive). Not everyone is wired to live in the glare of the spotlight. It's bright and hot and blinding…can you take it?

"**There came a time when the risk to remain tight in the bud was more painful than the risk to blossom.**" ~Anais Nin

"**Every single one of us knows heartache. It's the human condition. So do we settle for small dreams to make sure we can achieve them? Do we never test our will, our potential, for fear of failing?**" ~Diana Naiad, marathon swimmer

"**Success is going from failure to failure without loss of enthusiasm.**" ~Churchill

MIKE'S STILL TALKING:
"**Another way you can sabotage your Big Happy Life is by the negative use of RAS** (our old friend the Reticular Activating System). If you're always looking for negative things to appear, expecting a poor result, and if the worst case scenario is what you envision *first*, then you're training your brain to drag you down a dismal path. [Insert sound of you sinking in quicksand.] Maybe you think this point of view is true, because that's what your life looks like. Well, perhaps your life looks like a hot mess because that's what you've gone looking for! **Flip your**

perspective. Stand on your head if you can. Change the way you see the world and that will change your reality."

"Never let what you cannot do interfere with what you can do."
~John Wooden

"Aerodynamically the bumblebee shouldn't be able to fly, but the bumblebee doesn't know that so it goes on flying anyway."
~Mary Kay Ash

"I can be changed by what happens to me, but I refuse to be reduced by it." ~Maya Angelou

Keep a Box of Uplifts
Long ago Oriana overcame life-threatening chronic depression, and one of her tools to do that was something she calls her Box of Uplifts. It's a beautiful wooden box in which she keeps notes to herself about how fabulous she is. Some she writes herself, others are printed accolades that arrived as emails. Others are attagirl cards she's received in the actual U.S. mail—remember those days? (This is different from a gratitude journal or a keepbook of happy moments.) **This is all about YOU and how amazing you are!** It's a very private practice, not really meant to be shared, which encourages complete candor. This is not the time to be humble or reticent. Remind yourself in glowing terms precisely how ready-for-primetime-wonderful you know you are.

Happit: *applauding* **Create your own Box of Uplifts (or bag or cylinder or bucket) and add at least one accolade to it every day for those 21 all-important days.** This is quick to do and a deceptively simple tool, but one that can transform any gray day. Because everyone needs a boost now and then, delving into your Box of Uplifts will refocus your mind on what's true about you. **JOY-FILLED TWIST:** make one for someone you live with and add something new every day for 21 days, at which point let them take over. First you train your brain to remember how amazing this other person is—then you teach *them* to train their own brain to believe it! (A guaranteed relationship repair kit, at no extra charge!)

> "Joy is what happens to us when we allow ourselves to recognize how good things really are." ~Marianne Williamson

> "We don't know who we are until we see what we can do."
> ~ Martha Grimes

Do you need a map?

Who hasn't been lost somewhere, sometime? Not you? Well go to the head of the orienteering class. (No it's not a class in Asian cuisine. Go ahead and Google it…you might even take it up as a sport!) Whenever you set out on a journey to change your life—even in small ways—there's always the possibility you'll get sidetracked or lose your focus and not know what to do next. Those bright shiny objects over there can emit seductive beams of light. And sometimes you drown in your own details and lose your way. Of course, there are times when life really does intervene and hurl you down a different road. Or you waste your whole morning spanking a misbehaving computer, which starts you on a downward facing dog of a day. (Why has *dog* become a pejorative? There's another **distraction**. Repeat after me: I will not troll Wikipedia looking for the answer to that etymological conundrum.)

Pay careful attention to these moments, because these are the times when it's easy to take a break from pursuing your vision, or even worse—give up all together. Practice instilling a new happit, and after you master that, sticking to other kinds of new routines should come more easily. We hate to cloud up this sunshiny day by mentioning *discipline*, but honestly that's what it takes to happitize your life.

One trick is to learn to ask yourself when beginning any new activity: Does this move me closer to my Big Happy Life, or distract me from it? Oriana has a sign on her monitor that asks: *Is this the best* *use of my time?* That reminder has yanked her back from aimlessly wandering the aisles of eBay…the quest for an authentic 1940s bowl of cherries tablecloth can wait.

MIKE HAS MASTERED THIS TRICK TOO:
"I use this question to make every decision, whether large or small. I love it because it simplifies even complex issues to a yes or no answer. From the friends I choose, the people I associate with, to the media I consume—you name it—and I'll answer it by asking myself that deceptively simple question. A person or a thing or an event either adds to my joy or not. End of discussion."

Another tip to edge you back on track is to pick one tiny task you *know* you can finish and do that right now—NOW we tell you—just for the joy tickle you'll get from accomplishing something, no matter how insignificant it may seem. Each item you manage to conquer makes the next thing on your list that much easier. Then before you realize it, you're back home in your perky place. We keep lists of tasks that can be done in 15 minutes or less. That way, when we can grab a few extra minutes while the corn cooks or the towels tumble, we can be productive—instead of dribbling away that bit of time getting caught up on *waiting*. **And that is a happit in action!** If something is important to you, you'll find a way; if it isn't, you'll find an excuse.

> **"Opportunity is missed by most people because it is dressed in overalls and looks like work." ~Thomas Edison**

Life: some assembly required
You've just entered the No Whine Zone, where you do the work of creating Your Big Happy Life. Effort is not a four-letter word. How many more episodes of *Housewives Who Think They Can Sing / Cook / Dance / Run An Amazing Race For A Tiara* can you watch without

committing a felony? We've shown you umpteen ways to stretch your days further to implement these ideas. Starting to feel overwhelmed by all our splendid and intriguing suggestions? Relax. Really. Just relax. Take as long as you want to. You have the rest of your life to be happier. The road to success is dotted with many tempting parking places. However, the sooner you get cracking on it, the sooner we can stop nagging you.

> **"Small change, small wonders—these are the currency of my endurance and ultimately of my life." ~Barbara Kingsolver**

AFFIRMATIONS: I take some action every single day to expand the joy in my life. I implement my vision for my Big Happy Life and have boatloads (no metric equivalent available) of fun doing it. I know that real happiness comes from pursuing my dreams and I enjoy the thrill ride!

In the next chapter: We'll move on to all those other people in your life who may—or may not—be truly on Team You. If you think nobody cares whether you're flourishing or not, try missing a couple of payments.

Chapter Six
Enlarge Your Life
finding support for your vision

In this chapter:
- ✓ There's a test for that
- ✓ Just flip it
- ✓ Try this litmus test
- ✓ Assemble your joy team
- ✓ What to do with a broken widget
- ✓ Managing anger
- ✓ More is better
- ✓ The Nays don't have it
- ✓ What to do with pesky crows
- ✓ Put on your hazmat suit
- ✓ Have value to exchange

Let the sunshine in

Let's face it, as much as you may enjoy feeling independent and like being the captain of your own ship, having help along the way does make life easier. Especially if your happy vision entails a major overhaul of your life or changing direction or starting a new business, you need some great allies. In this chapter we'll help you to find good help (mentors, cheerleaders, coaches, advisors)—and perhaps throw a few not-so-helpful people overboard, figuratively speaking, of course. We'll also offer insights on spreading joy where you work, plus other tips for making Mary merry (or Waldo or Wanda). As that genius Anonymous said: "Those who bring sunshine to the lives of others cannot keep it from themselves."

MIKE SHARES SOMETHING COOL:

"I have my very own Happ-O-Meter that I use all the time. When I meet new people, (especially for job interviews) I ask them how happy they are on a one-to-ten scale. If someone says: 'Oh I'm about a three'…they don't realize they've already lost me, because I'm a twelve. They just aren't going to fit in my environment, because I'm an outrageous guy, and I want people I hire to have fun. I ask: *How do you spend your day? What books have you read lately? Do you ever read books on happiness? How important is it to have fun? What's your sense of humor like?*

Because I've had to overcome a lot of challenges, I've read everything I could get my hands on about positive thinking. **And I know as a rule of thumb that only a small percentage of people pursue self-improvement with any great zeal.** I want to hang out with like-minded people who enjoy other inspiring thinkers. When I enter a room I'm always looking for the person who's smiling and laughing and having the most fun. That's the one I want to meet.

I once asked a guy at a job interview: *What makes you different?* And he takes off his shoes to show me that he always wear two different colored socks. Now that made me laugh—and I hired him. **Remember:**

the people you surround yourself with are the employees of your LIFE."

What kind of impression do *you* make? How much time do you spend complaining, kvetching, gossiping or whining? If you're not sure, ask someone who knows you well—it may surprise you. Let's just suppose you spend 20 minutes a day in those activities. 20 minutes X 7 days = 2 hours and 20 minutes every week that could be transformed into much HAPPIER activities. That's about 10 hours a month or 120 hours a year you'd be spending NOT being happy! Sheesh! Just as every bite you eat during the day contributes to your caloric load, so does every negative moment contribute to your quality of life—or lack thereof.

Happit: *flipping* Monitor what comes out of your mouth daily for— you guessed it—21 days, and stop yourself from indulging in non- productive negative speak. (Giving someone constructive criticism is fine; griping about your boss and his pet aardvark is not. Well, perhaps if the aardvark bites you.) Every time you catch yourself about to whine or gossip, flip it around and find something positive to say instead. Nothing comes to mind? Then say nuthin'. Granny was right: if you can't say something nice, don't say anything. This sort of mindless negative speak really reduces your happiness, and on some level it makes you feel bad, too, whether or not you consciously relate it to what just spewed out of your apple pie hole. Be sure to taste your words before you spit them out!

> **"When someone does something good, applaud!
> You'll make two people happy." ~Samuel Goldwyn**

☺ **Make some cards to hand out:** *Congratulations! You've scored well on my personal Happ-O-Meter. I enjoyed our interaction, and hope you continue to spread joy wherever you go.* Leave cards with tips whenever people are helpful and extra pleasant; hand to someone who greets you warmly, give to someone you have a nice chat with on a plane, or leave on a check-out counter when you've been joyfully assisted. Think of all the happiness *you* can spread, one card at a time; **you never know what connection you might make, and it's certainly one way to make a memorable impression on someone.** Remember: the only really decent thing to do behind someone's back is pat it.

> **"The way is long, let us go together. The way is difficult, let us help each other. The way is joyful, let us share it."**
> ~Joyce Hunter

Human Litmus Test

Notice how you feel after interacting with someone—better or worse? After an unsettling encounter, instead of picking some coping mechanism like liquor, lambasting or linguini overload, stop and ask yourself if this is the kind of person you want in your life. You do have a choice!

MIKE SAYS:

"Make a list of everyone you interact with, no matter how insignificant you think they are in your life. You'd be surprised how big an impact casual exchanges can have on your day. Yes, it IS worth waiting for your favorite checker to avoid a downer experience. Take some time to see if there are areas where you can improve the quality of your days by finding more compatible people to deal with. Even churches can be sources of negativity—I've switched churches several times looking for people who actually walk the talk and genuinely care about those around them, rather than just appearing to. **If you leave the presence of someone and you don't feel joyful, then that's a real sign of trouble.** Which kind of person do you want in your life? It's never too late to assemble your own big happy family, your very own **Joy Team**. Surround yourself with positive thinkers who DO believe in your dreams."

**"No one can whistle a symphony. It takes an orchestra to play it."
~H.E. Luccock**

We all have support networks, but think beyond your friends to all the other people you interact with: your barber or hairdresser, manicurist, a gardener, your massage therapist, a housekeeper, childcare helpers, a chiropractor, the dry cleaner, your vet, the mechanic, your unicycle dealer. **All these people are in your life because you selected them, and you're paying for their services.** So if any of them are taking you on a downward joy-less-ride, then it's time to rethink who you hire to help you. Ideally all the people in your life participate in a joy exchange—they bring happiness to you and you return it to them (big red bow optional).

Many people amble through life accumulating friends in a random manner and never stop to analyze the troupe they've assembled. Even fewer people make a concerted effort to recruit specific kinds of people into their life, which is exactly what Mike did. **He knew he needed mentors, so he went out and found some. So can you.**

"Everyone you meet comes with some baggage. Find someone who loves you enough to help you unpack." ~Wise Aunt Wilma

☺**Clown Wisdom:** Think of the warmest, cheeriest person you know, even if it's not someone you know well. Now imagine that *everyone* in your life shares similar qualities of exuberance, good naturedness and playfulness. **Visualize all the people in your inner circle acting as a supportive, uplifting network of joy.** Sounds great, doesn't it? Well, the good news is it's very attainable, if you set that intention for yourself. On that list of the people in your life, identify ones who are positive enough to remain on your Joy Team and ones who may need some coaching or even be nudged out the door. How many Donald Downers can you afford on your team? *None?* Good answer! Thomas Edison, when asked why he had a team of twenty-one assistants: "If I could solve all the problems myself, I would."

You broke my widget? That's hysterical!

The people you spend the most time with are probably your co-workers, so being surrounded by happy campers is crucial to your overall joy level. Mike knows this well. When things go wrong at work, he believes in turning the situation upside down and somehow finding humor in it. When the water main bursts or the printer goes kaflooey, what's done is done…you can't unburst it or unkafloo it, so you might as well have a laugh over it and reduce the tension in your workplace. **Mike has perfected the art of viewing unexpected obstacles as opportunities for optimism.**

- ★ People make mistakes—*you burned how many unfortuneate cookies?* Who wants some garden mulch?
- ★ People lose things—*you misplaced the distribution list?* Now's a perfect time to create a new list but do it even better, organize it by zip code or tattoo placement.
- ★ People forget how to do things—*you put my sweater in the dryer and shrunk it?* Well let's shrink it some more until it fits the schnauzer!

The point is anger accomplishes nothing, and making someone who already feels bad feel worse won't unburn the cookies. The next time something goes awry: stop, count to ten (or twenty if you're really steamed) and ask yourself: **Will anger solve this problem or contribute anything to the discussion?** Big Hint: the answer is almost always NO!

Neuroscientists using MRIs can prove that when you think angry thoughts or other negative ideas, your blood whooshes into the areas of your brain connected to depression and anger. That in turn amps up your anger even more in a truly vicious circle. As this pattern continues, you saturate your body with stress hormones which proceed to wreak their own havoc, diminishing your ability to reason well.

The good news is that the opposite is also true: **think happy thoughts and good things happen in your noggin:** those neural superhighways become more robust, you relax and are better able to use your brainpower to make good choices.

Mike also knows from his extensive research and study of other successful companies that your team is your competitive edge, that the attitude of your staff can make you or break you, and their happiness is paramount in that equation. **Which is why he does everything he can think of to motivate and inspire his employees to excel—and have fun doing it.**

**"You're never angry for the reason you think you are.
Below anger is pain and below that is love." ~Iyanla Vanzant**

**"Work is either fun or drudgery.
It depends on your attitude. I like fun." ~Colleen Barrett**

MORE STUFF MIKE SAID:

"As the **CEO** of Fancy Fortune Cookies I take my title seriously… but I think of myself as the **Chief Energy Optimizer**. That means I have to help my people optimize their attitude during the day—especially when things go off the rails. I try and think of things to do that will give them an energy boost, which is really needed when we have huge orders to get out. Another title I take seriously is **CHO** (which I have on my business cards). That's **Chief Humor Officer**, and I love being the silly guy who cracks up my team when they need it most. I'll go get treats for everyone then run into the bakery ringing a bell and scream *ice cream break*. To prank or not to prank…*really, you had to ask?* Yes is my answer! I love to answer our order line as a funny character or use some goofy accent, which always astounds my actual customer service reps. By now they're used to having calls handed over to them from me after

I've pretended to be Sally or Sanjay or Mr. Sudoku. The last title I like to use is **HHH** or **Head Happiness Honcho**. It's my job to ensure that all the people in my life have a happier day. Sometimes I'll order pizzas at lunch for everyone, or I might set up a dart board at a staff meeting and tell them they're going to get a bonus at the end of the week based on the highest number they hit with a dart. Other times I've sent key team members on a cruise to reward them for their hard work and loyalty.

What keeps me going after 24 years is that this is a fun product, and I have fun with them. Fortune cookies are really little happiness devices. When I do trade shows, people are always amazed at our product, and they're always astonished that our cookies really do taste like the fruit they're made from. I love spreading happiness with my products. **No matter what your dream or vision is for Your Big Happy Life, I challenge you to live it in a way that also brings happiness to others."**

"The supreme accomplishment is to blur the line between work and play." ~Arnold Toynbee

Whether you're the boss or not, you can still spread happiness, you can be the most cheerful one in your office. Show that you care about co-workers' lives, be the rememberer of milestones, **become the happiness optimizer in your workplace**. Encourage more fun in your workplace…Plaid Day anyone? It can pay huge dividends, not just in raising your own happiness level, but in branding you as someone everyone wants on their team, as someone who makes coming to work less like, well, *work*.

The joy you spread goes farther than you imagine. Mike appreciates the happiness that comes from watching others enjoy his antics. He knows his staff likes to take home stories of his escapades, which is a sign his tactics are working. Every person who hears about his stunts also gets to share in the fun.

happit: *optimizing* By now you know the plan: for the next 21 days **find some way to optimize happiness among people on your Joy Team**, whether at work, at home or any other place your desires lure you. It can a tiny gesture (picking up an extra latte or your way to the office) or a grand one (picking up the spirits of a friend who's just suffered a major loss). Just consciously do something every single day. No fair searching back over your day looking for actions that fit this happit—**you must be aware of your action as you are doing it**. It needs to be *intentional* for this to create a new neural pathway through that noggin of yours.

☺ No matter how many fires you have to put out, never underestimate the power of a funny hat.

This is sad news: studies show that many people are more sociable, more engaged with people around them and happier *at work* than on their vacations! If this rings a bell for you, then you need some serious vaca-rehab. Life is too short to waste a vacation! You don't have to go far, or spend a lot of money to do something that creates more happy memories. Yes, cleaning out the garage and gutters are important, but so is expanding your life and joy through new experiences.

Do you know who's really on your team?
Everyone who has ever shared their dreams for a better life has eventually encountered naysayers—even when they're disguised as friends or family *who say they only want what's best for you*. Naysayers are like a mob of noisy crows heckling you from surrounding trees; they want to distract you and talk you out of pursuing your ideal life. There are many reasons why people close to you may not agree with your vision for Your Big Happy Life, let us count some ways: fear, jealousy, competitiveness, selfishness. It can be tough for some people to watch

someone else surge ahead and create a better life. **Some possible culprits:**
- Your mother-in-law, who worries that if you become too involved with grad school, you'll have less quality time for her son and your children.
- A friend who can't help being jealous of your desire to better yourself. Like a crow stealing berries right out of your garden, she pecks away at your plans, tearing them apart and eating away at your self-confidence.
- A colleague who fears change and wants to keep you on her level, where she never has to confront her own dead-end job.

If you're wavering at all in your goals and desires, all it may take is one arrow shot by a naysayer to pop your happy balloon. If you find yourself surrounded by them, then it may be time to upgrade your circle.

"A great pleasure in life is doing what people say you cannot do."
~Walter Bagehot

MIKE STAYED STRONG:
"Everyone who's successful has been hit upside the head by negativity, but they've learned to deal with it. I got lots of 'no's and lots of rejection as I started to market my fortune cookies, people who thought my ideas were crazy-bad. I even encountered jealousy among people I thought of as friends. You need to surround yourself with people who DO believe in your dream."

"How others treat me is their path; how I react is mine."
~Wayne Dyer

How do you handle these pesky crows? Remember, you rarely change naysayers into yeasayers, but **you do control how you respond to them**.

- ✓ First try and determine their motivation. If they really don't have your best interest at heart, then steer clear, especially when you're feeling vulnerable. Above all, stop sharing your dreams with them.
- ✓ Keep reminding yourself what you know is your truth, and turn away from their bad advice. Be firm. It's okay to reply to questions by saying, "You know, my plans aren't firm yet, so I won't go into them right now." Then change the subject.
- ✓ Your response may even need to be more drastic, even ending destructive friendships. What value is a friend who doesn't want for you your highest good?
- ✓ Perhaps you need to limit your exposure to family members who don't support your goals—at least until you've achieved them and are already living Your Big Happy Life.
- ✓ Don't engage your mirror neurons and return the acid—toxic behavior can be contagious (another one of those sciency findings). As tough as it might be, you need to be the better person. There is no joy in trying to make other people miserable, no matter how icktastically they've mistreated you.

The reality is, **if you allow naysayers to derail your vision, you give them your power—your power to improve your life and grow as a human being.** So just say NO to naysayers! People too weak to follow their own dreams will always find a way to discourage yours.

> **"You need to overcome the tug of people against you as you reach for high goals."** ~George S. Patton

☺**AFFIRM:** There is no room in my mind or my spirit for negative ideas; I turn each one away at my door. No one else has power over my thoughts; I am in charge of my own destiny—and it is glorious!

> **"No tree has branches foolish enough to fight among themselves."**
> **~Native American wisdom**

There are antidotes for this poison

One of the most important things you can do to increase your happiness is assess your life and take inventory of everything that makes you feel bad, of any negative influences you can find. Then one by one, work to eliminate them from your life. For instance, **toxic people have no place in your life.** (All naysayers are probably toxic, but not all toxic people express themselves as naysayers. Some are just plain mean or nasty or icky to be around.)

Think carefully about all the people in your life, especially ones you see often, and note the ones who drag you down rather than lift you up. You know they're toxic if being around them makes you feel a certain way you don't want to feel: sad, down or depressed, or they rekindle painful memories you'd rather forget. In that case, you want to do everything in your power to avoid them. It may involve tough love and not hanging out with them anymore. Sometimes these toxic people are family members, which can make deleting them from your life impossible, but you can work to minimize their impact and learn techniques to protect your own energy and mood when you're around them.

- Maybe it's just limiting the time you spend with them or the situations you get into with them.
- For some people, saving their sanity requires moving far away. Anyone can tolerate one annual visit to the family, no matter how stressful.
- Sometimes adding others to the mix as buffers can lessen the toxic impact.

It's your choice if you allow the same people to push the same hot buttons over and over. It's like the classic *SNL* routine with Billy Crystal and Christopher Guest as night watchmen who enjoy one-upping each other with tales of idiotic self-injury involving thumbtacks, carrot peelers and ball peen hammers. The payoff line is: *I hate when that happens.* 'Ya think?

Another potential source of toxicity in your life is your workplace. There are few things worse for your soul than spending the bulk your time in an environment that makes you feel bad. If you're working at a job you don't love, you might want to examine that. Life is too short to spend time with people who suck the happiness out of you.

> **"Tell me who your friends are and I'll tell you who you are."**
> **~Assyrian proverb**

MIKE HAS MORE TO SAY:
 "I can tell you there's nothing more magical than living your life, expecting you'll have fun that day. You want to wake up in the morning and be all excited, and you want to be so consumed by passion for this job that you'd pay someone else to let you do if you had to. That's the degree of intensity I'm talking about. Top performing athletes have that, as do all sorts of performers and artists. But so do people out of the public eye. Think about teachers or nurses or cupcake bakers you may have known who have that sort of zeal. That's when you know you're living at your highest level. **If every day you remove a little negativity out of your life, you will start to have a healthier and happier life."**

> **"A pessimist's blood type is always b-negative."**
> **~Dracula (and he ought to know!)**

If you have a toxic co-worker, much tact will be needed to navigate a resolution. But doing nothing about it is a surefire way to ruin most of your days (and evenings for that matter, as you rehash, gripe and whine about your aggravating co-worker). You don't have to burn your bridges all at once if that's too daunting. Just loosen the bolts a little each day.

 Other toxic influences might be your neighborhood or specific neighbors. Or perhaps it's the places you go on a regular basis, or even the type of music you listen to that drags you down. Try and monitor your mood as you go through your day and watch for moments when it shifts for the worse. What just happened? **Identifying all the toxicity in your life is the first step to removing it.**

Oriana is quite adept at ridding her life of toxic people and is thrilled to report there are NONE at all in her circle. She has made some trade-offs to achieve that, but it was the right decision for her. "Saying no to others meant saying yes to myself. I honor my own values and traditions without apology, which means I get to enjoy guilt-free, drama-free winter holidays of my own choosing. Ahhh."

Tell yourself that the coming week is a blank piece of paper. You can write about fear and doubt and negativity on it, or you can write about happiness. You decide.

☺ HAPPY ZAPPERS

Moderate/modulate/eliminate your media intake! Our brains are not really wired to absorb the constant onslaught of negativity that erupts on our screens 24/7. Eventually all we feel is angry or helpless or both—and both erode our precious quality of life. How many more fires, murders, floods, accidents and starlet tantrums do you need to hear about? Wouldn't you rather immerse yourself in joy?

> **"What do you pack to pursue a dream, and what do you leave behind?" ~Sandra Sharpe**

Be you, not them

Eliminating negative thinkers from your life frees up a lot of mental energy. Mike says: "I don't care what other people think about me—do you care what others think of you? Have you let it squelch your dreams? Be your own authentic self—that's who you were born to be." Stay strong in your uniqueness, it's what makes you special and different from everyone else. One of Oriana's favorite lessons was: "What you think of me is none of my business." And living that philosophy allowed her to dye her hair purple when she felt like it, to move to a Caribbean island when no one else thought it was a good idea, and to always wear comfortable shoes.

One way to protect your uniqueness is to brand yourself as a value exchanger—someone who always adds extra value to each encounter. That way, when you need to ask a member of your Joy Team for help, they're eager to give it, because they're already witnessed your own generosity. What might you offer? In a macadamia shell, it's a new way of viewing your interactions with almost everyone—even when you can't foresee there being something in it for you. **Brand this:** Be so happy that when others see you, they become happy, too.

AFFIRMATION: I enlist others and leap forward into my Big Happy Life. I attract other positive thinkers to help me and join me on my joy-filled path. I am becoming everything that I was born to be, and I'm having a blast along the way.

In the next chapter:
By golly you did it—you reached the three-ring finale! Become the life of your party, stop worrying and start dancing, see what kids have to teach us, take gratitude to new dimensions and join the movement. C'mon!

Chapter Seven
Celebrate Your Big Happy Life
multiplying your joy

In this chapter:
- ✓ Most things are worth less than you think they are
- ✓ The life of the party—is that you?
- ✓ Say it out loud
- ✓ Silly is good
- ✓ Kids make the best teachers
- ✓ Make your gratitude real
- ✓ Get outta town!
- ✓ Crank up the music
- ✓ Pass it on
- ✓ Finding humor where there shouldn't be any

In the last chapter we examined the people in our lives and maybe even ditched a few! In this final chapter we'll look at ways to expand the amount of joy you can fit into Your Big Happy Life and how to increase the good vibes with your Joy Team.

☺ The more happiness you share, the more you have to enjoy yourself —you can't give it all away! What can you teach others, how might you pass on some wisdom to people who need your expertise? Offer yourself. Volunteer. Be of service. The joy you'll be paid in is priceless!

MIKE ON BLISS:

"After so many years of being a student, I realized it was time to give back and become a teacher. I spent decades learning how to start and run a business, to be a positive thinker and to experience maximum happiness in my life. Now I think of myself as a messenger of fun and happiness, and sharing what I've learned is a real blessing.

In speaking about joy all over the world, it's been easy to see a central theme and question: *How can I have more fun and infuse my life with more joy?* My first answer is always: If you're just trying to see how much money you can make, you won't find joy; **you need to shift your desires to experiences, not things.**

One way I get to have so many joy-filled experiences is through my friends. I have pals who are millionaires and even a billionaire, so I've seen extreme wealth up close and personal. We enjoy talking business, but what they appreciate about me most is that I'm always the life of the party, always upbeat, always raising the energy of any room. So guess what? I get invited to fun places. People want me at their conferences just to jazz up the event. It's a bit like being a jester, getting invited because of the energy I bring, but that's fine with me, since I never take myself too seriously and I'm always willing to play the fool. Besides, I already have the hat for it."

☺There's no fool like an old fool…but some of you young fools are showing real promise. It's the Fool who we trust to tell us the truth. It's the Fool whose voice we believe.

☺**How to become the life of the party:**
- ☺ Ensure others have a great time.
- ☺ Be entertaining—tell jokes, play music, read tarot cards, dance a mean mambo.
- ☺ Be memorable, dare to be outlandish, wear something sparkly.
- ☺ Help serve food and drinks—an easy way to speak to everyone (which is your goal).
- ☺ Introduce people well—point out their common interest in squirrels who water ski.
- ☺ Don't have tee many martoonis—drunks are only funny on TV.
- ☺ Stay away from walls, own the center of the room.
- ☺ Be enthusiastic if the host suggests activities (of the legal variety).
- ☺ Encourage people to talk about their favorite topic—themselves! Take a genuine interest and don't be over-focused on your own agenda (unless it's a biz gathering, then go for it).
- ☺ Shameless plug: Mike takes personalized fortune cookies to events, a fun conversation starter.

Don't succumb to this buzz kill

If you're not invited to fun events, maybe it's because of what comes out of your mouth. No silly, your words. No one likes a sourpuss who drags dark clouds around or Dour Donna who drones on and on about the gloomy economy. In this era of uncertainty it's essential to take full responsibility for your financial well-being, because worrying about the economy is a recipe for UNhappiness and a shortcut to sleep loss. Shut your mind off from the pervasive fear people around you may be wallowing in.

A surefire way to replace lost happiness is to do something about your financial health. **You may even want to work extra hard for awhile just to build up some strong reserves**, to actually stockpile the six months' worth of living expenses that all the money mavens say you should have in the bank. You *will* sleep better at night and jack up your joy. *How can I do that, you ask?*

- Develop new streams of income online. Become an affiliate. Open an Amazon shop for All Things Gladiolas.
- Sell your crafts on Etsy.com. If you make hats for cats, they will come.
- Start a home business that might spin out of a hobby. The more fun it is, the more you're likely to put energy into it. Refinish furniture and hand paint zinnia gardens all over them. Reupholster vintage car seats—TuftsRus.com!
- What do you know how to do really well? Become a consultant and charge for your expertise on a freelance basis. With Skype and a webcam, the whole world is your client base.

Once you have yourself feeling more secure, **help other people to do the same and you WILL become the life of the party!** By far, Mike's favorite party accessory is his beautiful wife…

MIKE ON HAPPILY EVER AFTER:

"I waited a long time to get married, because I waited to meet the right woman. I was under pressure from about age 21 onward to marry (and all my prodders had been married multiple times). **I didn't want to get married three times. I wanted to be married ONE time.**

Luckily, I found my soul mate, and today Erin is such an important part of my life. Success and accomplishment mean so much more when you share it with a partner…it really amplifies everything you do and achieve. Erin understands how much it means to me every time I check off one of my life goals from my list. And now my wife is part of my company—which may not be for everyone—but for us, it works. I love it because we have good mojo, spend more time together and we get to enjoy the milestones of running a company together, like delivering our cookies to a charity event at Donald Trump's Mar-a-Lago estate. Happiness is so much richer when you can savor it with someone and relive over and over your magic moments.

Erin proved to me that it's never too late to bring more happiness into your life. No matter what age you are, keep looking for someone who loves you exactly as you are. Look for someone who complements your happy viewpoint—don't settle for someone who drains you and drags you down. Erin and I are always trying to identify things that make each other's heart sing…we work at infusing each other with happiness."

You may not realize what's missing from your life until you *do* meet your soul mate. **Mike is determined to respect and appreciate everything Erin does for him.**

- He tries to remember to **tell her every single day** that he *genuinely* loves her.
- He leaves little **love notes** hidden all over the house, especially if he's going out of town. He likes to match them to where he hides them: *Wish I was there* is left on her pillow. *Love is the best medicine* inside the medicine cabinet. *Have I told you lately how cool you are?* goes in the freezer. *Your love is priceless to me* waits in her wallet. *Lucky lipstick* is taped to, well, you can figure that one out, Sherlock. Besides sending her love, of course he wants to make her laugh!
- Every Friday is their **date night**…it doesn't have to be a fancy outing…it's about spending superior time together. Aim for the unexpected: a canoe, miniature golf, a planetarium, poetry slam, midnight movie, a horseback ride, a make-your-own-pottery-vase class, rent a bicycle built for two, go through a haunted house, slosh around a waterpark. The goal is to create new HAPPY memories, not have another routine burger at the same-old place. Besides, new activities keep your relationship fresh.

❋Make your partner feel special, **take an interest** in what excites them. Create common ground even where none might exist on its own. Even if you don't love Monday Night Football or spinning class or the finer points of pruning bonsai, make an effort to understand what makes your partner enjoy it and find a way to share it with them from time to time.

Happit: *declaring* Tell someone you love them for 21 days in a row. It might be your spouse, another family member or a friend—mix it up—*who* it is is less important than your saying it daily. No writing this time, the magic words must be spoken aloud, which is great practice for the shy and repressed (and you know who you are!).

MIKE ON PARENTHOOD:

"I can't talk about happiness unless I talk about my daughter Ella, who just turned four. She loves to ride on my shoulders and I pretend to be her horse. From the age of two I taught her circus tricks…lifts and tumbling and balancing…and we love playing together like that. I walk around with her standing on my shoulders (but don't try this at home). **I never thought about how much fun it would be to have my own child.** By age three she already understood simple jokes, and she'd look at me to be sure I got it that she was telling a joke. Ella was already learning comedic timing and the value of humor (even though the concept of a punch line may have eluded her). She really is wild, fun and crazy—just like her doting dad. Every single day I try to instill fun and happiness into her life. **I never want Ella to think I'm too grown up to act like a kid again and play with her,** and she shows me how to reach even new levels of fun and silliness. You're never too old to be young.

One of Ella's friends came over to the house and he wanted one of her toys. At first she didn't want to give it up, but then I encouraged her to give it to him by reminding her of a time when someone shared something with her. I told her how good it would make her feel to share with her friend. So she did, and big smiles ensued.

It's critical that she understand how to find happiness and what makes her feel good. **I want to teach her from a young age to be grateful and generous, because those are key building blocks of a human being.** While we're driving around town together I'm always asking her: *Who's the most creative, positive, caring little girl in the world?* It took awhile, but now she knows the answer is: *Ella!* All the affirmations that I repeated daily to her while she was in the womb, are values I continue to instill in her now that she's old enough to understand them."

☺One of my favorite things is that we built a hut in my office and filled it with animals. We play zoo, we play vet, whatever she wants to do. **The value of silliness is releasing adult cares and stress.** So if there are any children in your life, see if you can't let go more and regress back to their level.

"Adults are always asking little kids what they want to be when they grow up because they're looking for ideas." ~Paula Poundstone

☺Record happy times, since childhood memories fade. Write down the silly things they do—you will *both* forget them—and they'll mean so much later on. You may even be surprised at the wisdom they contain. **You're never to old to learn something from a child.** As Mike recalls: "We went on a cruise and I knew my daughter was going to see the ocean for the very first time, so I went prepared to document the whole event. I took pictures and video and made notes about how she reacted and what I saw in her eyes. The very first time she walked barefoot in the sand and picked up a crab—those moments are so magical. And I still do the same thing for myself. I don't take for granted any of the exciting new experiences I get to enjoy either.

My thing is: if Ella says: *Come on Daddy*…then I want to do whatever she wants to do. If it makes my daughter happy then I want to do it. More often than not, it's something other dads probably wouldn't do."

"Try to be a rainbow in someone's cloud." ~Maya Angelou

Many of us live with people who are real life exemplars of joyful living, people who ooze happiness every single day—children! **As Mike learned, there's a lot children can teach us.** If there are no children in your life, think about finding ways to interact with them—you'll be repaid in spikes on your Happ-O-Meter. **Here are some of his takeaways:**

* be interested in everything around you—*especially stuff close to the ground*
* be eager to play in the mud or paint—*clothes can be washed*
* be ever ready to smile—*someone might see it*
* be easily amused and entertained—*any insect will do*
* be willing to try new things, even things you think you shouldn't—*walk a low tightrope between two backyard trees for a fun empowerment exercise*
* be sure of yourself and your talents—*your drawings are Fridge-worthy*
* be willing to start new friendships—*new people stir the pot of your life*
* be willing to let go and let good take over after a spat—*who cares who saw the cashmere sweater on sale first?*
* be idealistic and trusting—*the Tooth Fairy is worth believing in*
* be free with your emotions, especially the good ones—*laughter is a wonderful gift*
* be ready to share your toys with others—*how many iPads do you need?*

✱ **be unashamed**—*be willing to look stupid / silly / magenta / polka-dotted or be seen with a duck on your head*

We don't really need to grow up, we only need to learn how to act in public.

MIKE MAKES CENTS OF GRATITUDE:
"That's not a typo, but it is sobering. Whenever I think about the importance of gratitude in my life, I remember this story. In America it can be so easy to take our quality of life for granted. A few years ago I was in Shenzhen, China, a city of about 11 million people, speaking at an event for Linda Chandler. As I drove to meet her, I saw about 300 people collecting old bricks and scraping the mortar off them with pieces of scrap metal. When I asked what they were doing, my interpreter said they were cleaning up after a building that was torn down, and they'd be paid for each brick cleaned. So I asked how much they'd earn in a day. After some calculations, he replied that for a 10-hour day, they'd earn about 12 American *cents*. That tiny amount gave me plenty to contemplate, and it's always stayed in my mind. How petty our concerns seem when compared with that equation. **Finding outlets for your compassion is a sure route to more joy in your life.**"

"Genuine happiness comes not from what we get from the world, but from what we give to the world." ~Alan Wallace

Let's get physical
Your life is the most exclusive and beautiful event you'll ever attend. And you ARE grateful for it, aren't you? Sure you are. By now everyone has heard about writing a regular gratitude journal, which when you keep it up, can indeed increase your happiness, boost your immune system, reduce stress and grow hair where you want it. Plus it's instructional to reread it and see how your life has evolved. But you won't be surprised, will you, if **we offer a BIGGER way to carry out**

this practice? Good. Here goes. You can still write down one or more things you're grateful for each day if you like, then pick one that feels most meaningful at that moment. **Next, figure out some way to make your act of gratitude *physical*.**

- ♣ If today you're most grateful for your home, then take time to demonstrate that by taking special care of it: do a chore you've been putting off, clean your gutters, plant some begonias.
- ♣ If it's your dog you're most grateful for today: show her some extra love—prepare a treat of pumpkin and carrots, or go for an extra, extra long walk, or fit in *two* games of b-a-l-l. (Can't say that one out loud unless you mean it!)
- ♣ If it's your job you're grateful for: then *tell* your boss you are and really mean it. Find a way to prove it—do something extra just because you can. It will have way more impact coming out of the blue instead right before evaluation time.

This idea illustrates the notion that actions speak louder than words. It's fine to make gratitude lists with colorful pens in pretty journals and feel content about Your Big Happy Life, but **we encourage you to *prove* your gratitude to the Universe by taking action**, by making your gratitude tangible. And we doubt this will surprise you: **you're bound to feel happier in the process**, as happiness is the natural result of appreciation. **Action always trumps thought.**

Need more examples? Sure! Love your view? Clean up the beach. Appreciate your kind neighbor Nancy? Do a chore for her that you suspect needs doing. Grateful for your recovery from a health scare? Take even better care of yourself—have a green smoothie. Have two. **Extra points for doing these activities with conscious intention, with awareness of your gratitude as you do them.** Got it? Good! Now go make some intangibles more touchy-feely.

"The secret of happiness is to count your blessings while others are adding up their troubles." ~Oprah

Happit: *thanking* Once a day for…how long?...yep, 21 days, write someone a thank you note and mail it or hand deliver it. It must be in writing on actual paper, or bark, or perhaps in the sand if you've got a beach and a big stick. Want to go BIG? Hire a skywriter! Take out a personal ad. (No, a flippin' email doesn't count. Nor does a tweet or a poke or a pin. Pick up a pen before you forget how!) Bonus points if you thank 21 different people. No fair thanking the same person over and over for the same thing, no matter how grateful you are for the shiny new kidney. Well, maybe that's the exception that breaks the rule.

> **"Those who bring sunshine into the lives of others cannot keep it from themselves." ~Sol**

☺ According to those who study such things: **two primary obstacles to gratefulness are: forgetfulness and a lack of mindful awareness**, and visual reminders can trigger a gratitude practice. So take a moment to tape some reminders where you'll see 'em. Because there's always something to be thankful for. For example, right now we're thinking how nice it is that wrinkles don't hurt. One great result of increasing your happiness levels via gratitude is that you'll get a lot more done. Happy people are just more productive. (Maybe it's all that time we save not whining, nagging and pestering.)

Go away!

Many people spend more time planning a vacation than they do planning their life. It just never occurs to them to be strategic, so they leave the course of their lives to chance. **Having no plan is a bad plan!**

Twice a year Mike goes on a personal development getaway. With a goal of spontaneity, he randomly grabs a bunch of tapes and CDs from his collection on goal setting, marketing and motivation to listen to while he drives, plus a stack of books. He sets off not knowing how far he's going and just drives until he gets tired or inspired by something he sees.

At the hotel he sets up his work space. His agenda is to generate ideas and goals for the next six months. Mike begins by reviewing how he did with his goals for the last six months. Sometimes he goes back in time as much as a year or two to look for trends. **The point is to *upgrade* his Big Happy Life.**

OUT OF MIKE'S MOUTH:

"The next morning I start by writing down everything I'm grateful for, things big and small—sometimes hundreds of things. I list the failures, too, because I'm also grateful for what I learn from them.

Then I start to develop my game plan, looking for ways to improve the quality of my life even more. Clarity come from analysis and writing out your vision. You can't keep this stuff in your head. Writing makes your thoughts accessible at any time in the future, makes your goals quantifiable and gives a way to track your progress. **This isn't some airy fairy exercise where you fantasize about how your life might look if magical things happen. This is a real strategy session.**

Then I start sketching out action steps. Doing the gratitude list reminds me what makes my heart sing, and it inspires me to include more of those activities in my schedule. For the next several days I just keep churning out ideas until I feel I have them all on paper and am ready to come back to daily life."

We encourage you to create your own version of this planning getaway, even if you can't get out of town. There's something powerful about a change of scene that opens your mind to new ideas. Try turning off your phone and camping in your backyard if you have to, borrow a friend's house while she's out of town, or trade homes with a pal.

Things to take:
- ☑ music that inspires you and puts you in a good mood or albums of nature sounds if you'll need to mask other noises

- ☑ input from thought leaders in your area of interest (but don't spend all your time reading other people's ideas—this is time to generate your own!)
- ☑ a copy of your vision for Your Big Happy Life
- ☑ huge sheets of paper to map your ideas without limits, colorful pens and markers to diagram your ideas
- ☑ an oracle (animal wisdom cards, tarot cards, the I Ching, runes) in case you need a tie breaker or a shove outside your own preconceptions
- ☑ things to change/create an exceptional space—candles, sage, celebratory cowbell, a quilt, extra pillows, flowers—whatever inspires you and reminds you this is not an ordinary day
- ☑ something to wear that makes you feel special: a necklace, monkey suit, grandpa's pocket watch, or even a goofy hat (always Mike's fave)

Oriana does these visioning trips too, only she prefers "day camping" in an inspiring setting—perhaps a national park—and spends a long day doing the same kind of work that Mike does, except she sleeps in her own bed every night. Then the next day she picks a different destination. **She likes to do her thinking in places with pristine air—** the mountains, forests, by the ocean or a lake and especially waterfalls—all of which contain tens of thousands of beneficial negative ions. She can actually count the number of ideas per hour she gets in those places and knows how much higher that number jumps when she works outdoors.

So go already!

"You can't expect insights, even the big ones, to suddenly make you understand everything. But I figure: Hey, it's a step if they leave you confused in a deeper way." ~Jane Wagner

> "You can't go back and start a new beginning,
> but you can start a new ending." ~Maria Robinson

If you're happy and you know it, say so!

On the surface, seeking Your Big Happy Life may seem a bit self-centered, though in fact, **the ultimate goal is to spread happiness to others**—but first you have to have plenty to share! Marianne Williamson writes, "As we let our own light shine, we unconsciously give other people permission to do the same." That's one of the great benefits of figuring our how to be happier—it affects everyone in your orbit and can't help but improve their lives, too.

Mike never misses an excuse for a party, and we hope you won't either. **Vow to celebrate every milestone you can think of, events large and small, serious and silly:**

- a stellar (or improved) report card
- daffodils bloomed today—the ones you planted to honor your mom
- the anniversary of the day you adopted your pug, Pong
- family talent show during an annual camping trip
- watching the Leonids meteor shower and saying an affirmation each time you see one arc across the heavens
- holding a Gratitude Festival for close friends at the time of the Harvest Moon
- Overcoming key fears and mental roadblocks with a symbolic action—skydiving anyone?
- Congratulating yourself for achieving interim goals with significant rewards—a leather-bound journal, a pampering spa day, a session with a life coach
- Finding new ways to celebrate winter holidays that add meaning to your lives, rather than stress—that'll add some joy to your world!

Celebrating some of the same milestones every year creates family traditions, which creates the magic emotional epoxy that bonds people together. And hey, when you happen to notice you're living Your

Big Happy Life, throw yourself a great party, too! Happiness is like jam. You can't spread even a little without getting some on yourself.

Do something today that your future self will thank you for.

> **"It is not easy to find happiness in ourselves, but it is not possible to find elsewhere."** ~Agnes Repplier

We're in this together

We live in a circular world: every smile you give away, every word of encouragement you offer, enriches your own life in full return. There's a kind of giddiness that can arise when your own happiness fills you so much that it spills over onto everyone you meet. If you aren't used to being that way in the world, it may seem counter-intuitive to focus more on other people's happiness (especially when you're in hot pursuit of more of your own). **But trust us, that is indeed one guaranteed ride on the up escalator.**

The poet John Holmes wrote: "There is no exercise better for the heart than reaching down and lifting people up." We like that because it shows how you both benefit from a good deed. Sadly, American life has lost so much civility in recent years, partly a result of the acrimonious political divide in the country. Bad-mannered talking heads on TV spew so much vitriol that it has seeped into our consciousness as acceptable behavior. That needs to stop. **We're calling for a return to kindness, cooperation and celebrating the goodness in people.** No act of kindness, however small, is ever wasted.

We challenge you to volunteer more, to pause to give directions to a stranger, to help your neighbors—even the ones you can't stand—*especially* the ones you can't stand, as that's an opportunity to reverse that trend. Reach out to newcomers, get involved in making your town better, be a vital part of your spiritual community, share your skills, find unconventional ways to share joy. In the small town closest to Oriana, a group of spirited artists do regular "yarn bombing": they wrap park benches, lamp posts and other street furniture in rainbows of bright fibers, transforming the mundane into art. Pure magic!

What tomfoolery might you get up to?

"Happiness held is the seed; happiness shared is the flower."
~Beaucoup Bouquets

☺**Our challenge to you:** See how much joy you can spread in one whole day—you can't deplete your stockpile of it, your soul will just make more.

"Seek to do good and you will find that happiness
will run after you." ~J. Clarke

"When you do things from your soul,
you feel a river running   through you, a joy." ~Rumi

"To get more out of life, give more of yourself." ~Amy Liao

Happy happens even in a hospital bed

We're not going to end this book on a downer, but Mike has had his happiness philosophy put to the ultimate test in 2001 and 2012. As if by a bolt from the blue, Mike was zapped by a hereditary genetic disease he didn't know he had. One day he's frolicking in the Caribbean with his fam, and the next he's fighting for his life, nearly drained of all his blood. Talk about running on empty!

MIKE EXPLAINS:

"There's nothing like three near-death episodes in one year to put your life in perspective. **I can either think of it as having a life threatening illness, or I can be grateful and supremely happy that I wake up each new day.** I pick the latter. I'm living, not dying. While

I've always cherished my family, this experience deepens our bond even more. I've certainly cried over my situation, not feeling sorry for myself, but worrying how Ella and Erin would cope. Erin has been so amazing running the cookie business by herself. It helps me to know how strong she is. One thing is for sure: I want to make the most of whatever time I have. I'm living proof that you never know what any day will bring, so you'd better jam pack the joy into every single one you get. **There is abso-stinking-lutely ZERO TIME to waste on petty, crappy, negative thoughts and actions!** *None. Zippo.* I hope you don't have to go through what I did in order to believe me. If you get nothing else out of this book, take that to the bank, where you can make withdrawals of daily joy. Though I'm not out of the woods—in fact I've built myself a charming log cabin in the woods—I'm savoring my Big Happy Life as much as I can. If you feel like sending some good thoughts in my direction, I'll open my heart wide and say thanks, my friend."

True to form, Mike even found ways to have fun in the hospital, as he recalls: "The day I learned I had cancer, I decided that I would be the happiest patient they had. So before we went into the doctor's office to discuss treatment options, I decided I was going to do the most fun thing possible. I didn't want to go in there all sad, so I went and got a wheelchair and planked myself right across it. That was almost too much for Erin, but she laughed and captured the moment with her camera, jumping right in to my joy plan."

**"To live is the rarest thing in the world.
Most people just exist." ~ Oscar Wilde**

**"You don't get to choose how you're going to die, or when.
You can only decide how you're going to live now."
~Joan Baez**

All clowns exit running
That's a classic reference to how the circus ends...wacky, chaotic and silly. We hope you've found ideas in this book—wacky and otherwise—to help welcome more happiness into your wide open soul. We want *you* to run full tilt into your fantastic, magical Big Happy Life…clown shoes optional.

But we can't let you go without a BIG FINISH: If you *are* inspired by our ideas (and the visions you've created for yourself) we challenge you to join our mission to spread happiness to others by instigating **Happy Happenings.** Be a catalyst who creates joy out of thin air (and perhaps some confetti). Every day is an opportunity to make a new happy ending. Examples are:

- You pick an armful of flowers from your garden, then hand them out one by one to strangers during your lunch hour.
- If you're musically talented, you entertain in unexpected places without accepting money for it.
- You gather a few friends to bring supplies to an animal shelter.
- You feed someone's expired parking meter
- You offer to babysit for free for a working mom.

After each of these actions, you could hand out or leave behind a simple card: You've experienced a Happy Happening. Spread the joy!

> "Don't be afraid your life will end; be afraid it will never begin."
> ~Grace Hansen

Affirmation: I rejoice in this perfect new day that I have never met before—it's a gift to be unwrapped then shared. I celebrate milestones of progress along my way and express my gratitude at every opportunity. I cherish the Big Happy Life I am creating, and I share my process with others. I seek ways to raise the happiness level of everyone I meet. I am glad to be alive!

> **"May you live all the days of your life."** ~Jonathan Swift

Afterword

By Erin Fry

Why a Big Happy Life?

At the end, when you breathe your last breath, all you leave behind are your actions, the memories and feelings created by the choices you make. Doesn't it make sense to engineer our life to have as many joy-filled, exciting, loving moments as possible!?!?! Isn't that how we will remember the people who go before us, and be remembered by those we leave behind? Each day you wake up you choose - You are going to live that day, it is up to you to live it with apathy or to live it with Happy.

I will never wake up pain free. The loss of my friend, partner in life and business, husband, father and love will always be with me. But I also know life is short and we only get this one shot at life. So each day I will get up and make today a great day.

I hope you will too.

HAPPITIONARY

Careful—these can be happit-forming!

To make this easy-peasy, we've collected all the happits in this book in one handy dandy place, so now you have no excuse when you want to find one. No matter how skeptical you may be (still?)…please give this idea a try. A really good try.

Happit: *anticipating* No, that's not a typo…we just crunched "happy habit" and got *happit*, which feels more fun and less tiresome to achieve. **Every day for the next 21 days find something to anticipate**, even if it's just leaving work a bit early or having something special for dinner. Do try though to schedule some longer term activities, so you can practice anticipating them again and again. Lavish some time on this—that's the whole point—the time you spend in delicious anticipation IS the joyful payoff.

Why 21 days? because another Harvard whiz determined that **it only takes 21 days of consistently doing something new to make it a habit for life.** After 21 days your shiny new happits will become automatic—how glad-making is that? Let's hear a whoop of joy for that one. The operative word in the formula is *consistently*—**if you skip a day you have to start over**—so set up a tracking system of some sort to help you attain that goal on your first go-around.

As with most of the happits you'll find in this book, you'll be way more apt to stay with them if you write them down and track them. You're going to hear this more than once from us, so get over it: **there is no way to overstate the immense value of journaling**. Journals act as time capsules so you can see the person you used to be—and appreciate the person you've become. You don't have to be a "writer"—this is not about creating literature, it's about preserving key facets of your life and recording the trajectory of it. Besides, you'll be amazed how useful journaling can be when you have a problem to solve. Writing out your thoughts can really help sort out your priorities and guide you toward resolutions. Besides, putting your thoughts on paper is a proven mood shifter. *Just do it!*

Happit: *finding time* Every day for those magical 21 days, consciously change your behavior, and instead of doing some distracting activity, spend at least ten minutes thinking about your happiness level and what you might do to improve it. You might spend the time with your Joy Tracker chart or yes—journaling. (*We warned you we'd nag you about this!*) For bonus points, track how much extra time you gather and put to better use.

Happit: *slowing* Try this every day for 21 days before you dismiss the idea. You might be amazed at the impact a few extra minutes can make. Get up 10-15 minutes earlier and plan ahead how to use the time well.

Happit: *repairing* For 21 days straight make an appointment at least once a day to check in on your mood. If it needs fixing, do whatever it takes to turn your emotional ship around. No rat-ass ugly days allowed!

Happit: *capturing* One solution is to learn to consciously notice these simple daily delights and slow down long enough to really experience them. To say *Yes, this makes me happy. This is why I (fill in the blank) every day. This makes life worth living.* You do this by developing self-awareness, by easing up your pace and becoming alert to joy in all its forms. Then once you train yourself to spot and relish these flashes of happiness, **the next step is to capture them**. If you don't think of yourself as creative, then besides being a lie because we're ALL creative, this part may sound like too big a project. But in fact, it's an essential part of living a Big Happy Life.

Capturing your happy moments may be as simple as jotting down a few sentences each night that help you remember the high points of your day. Or it may be as elaborate as creating a full-on multi-media scrapbook of your life. There is no way to emphasize enough how much value these efforts will have in later years as you—and your loved ones if you so choose—review these joyful times and relive them all over again. It can be enormously instructive to your family members to see what you've valued in your life, what has enriched your time here. These records of your life can become permanent keepsakes that document the Technicolor texture of your Big Happy Life. However you decide to capture your happy moments, be sure to do so for 21 days in a row.

Happit: *shifting* Practice shifting your thinking at least once a day for 21 days, from a negative assumption or point of view to a more positive one.

Happit: *cheer up* **Consciously demonstrate a different aspect of yourself in a more cheerful manner every day for 21 days straight.** Wear brighter colors, a flower in your lapel, a silly button, a Daffy Duck watch, a wacky hat, or even just a colorful pocket handkerchief if you work in one of those repressed offices. Or one day you might bring a vase of dahlias to work, or a homemade lemon meringue pie, or recycle a box of books and magazines with your co-workers. Perhaps you make a fuss over your neighbor's birthday or organize a book group lunch at a nicer-than-usual bistro. It matters not what you do, just that you demonstrate a happier state of being in some way every day, no two days the same. What will amaze you (and that's a promise) is the effect this will have not just on you, but on everyone you come into contact with. Like a pebble tossed into water, your cheerfulness will radiate outward and affect all the inhabitants of your metaphorical pond.

Happit: *belonging* **Find some kind of group to join.** We're social animals, and even the loners among us need some socializing. Belonging to a group—even if it only gathers once a month—delivers the same amount of happiness as doubling your income! Plus it's a great way to find allies, mentors and mastermind partners. If the purpose of the group is altruistic, you can get an even bigger boost by helping other people. **There is only ONE thing the happiest people all over the world have in common: they enjoy broad and deep personal support networks.** One of the best ways to enlarge yours is to join some groups of like-minded people. Then try this challenge: **Every day for the first 21 days after you find a group you like, do at least one thing to stay engaged with the group.** Call someone in the group, email a leader with thanks, have lunch with a new pal, volunteer to be on a committee, attend every function, offer to bring some healthy snacks, and so on.

Happit: *listening* **Monitor your thoughts and words.** Listen to yourself—how often do you use negative words, how often do you criticize, gossip or otherwise spread bad vibes? Mom was right: If you can't say something good about someone, shut your pie hole. How hard are you on yourself? Do you dismiss your own ideas before they even poke their heads out of the ground? Ridding your vocabulary of downer words and phrases can allow a lot more sunshine in your soul. For 21 days straight (no cheating) keep a written record of at least one incident a day when you correct yourself and flip your words in a better direction.

Happit: *naturing* **Bring the outside in every day.** For 21 days without interruption, go outside and choose at least one object to bring home. (Preferably not roadkill.) It can be a pine cone from your yard, a crow feather you find on the sidewalk, a colorful stone you trip over. What it is or where you collect it is not the real point—it's getting outside and paying closer attention to your environment that matters most. Extra credit for making a work of art out of all 21 objects at the end of the three weeks. For even more fun, involve kids or friends…have a scavenger hunt. Or go for 26 days and look for things that reflect every letter of the alphabet: apple, bone, cone, daffodil, echinacea, feather, and so on. (Make up your own rule for X!)

Happit: *smiling* **Make yourself smile every time you think of it all day long.** (It works better if you smile *at* someone, though the dog will work in a pinch. Not so sure about a goldfish.) You don't have to know the nice people or even like them, just grin anyway. Do not let one day go by without smiling for 21 days in a chirpy row. Smile at everyone, you never know who's an angel, or the Fairy Godfather you're about to meet. We live in a circular world: every smile you give away, every word of encouragement you offer, enriches your own life in full return. Be prepared to be bowled over like a teetering pin blasted by a Brunswick purple/blue Nexus ball when you see how people react to you once you master this happit. A smile is a curve that sets everything straight, and a smiling person brings happiness wherever they go.

Happit: *values* **Make a list of your most cherished values, things that add meaning to your life.** What values do you aspire to live by? What values cause you to do or *not do* certain things? For example, some of Mike's core values are: Fun, Friendship, Integrity, Spontaneity, Love, Sincerity, Passion, Honesty, Truth, Accomplishment. **Add at least one new value to your list every day for 21 days.** By the end of that time, thinking about your values (and consciously integrating them into your life) will become second nature. For instance, remembering that you value *spontaneity* can make you more apt to say yes to fun adventures rather than perpetuating old workaholic habits. *Elephant riding in Thailand? Sure!* Does your life reflect your values? If not, what needs to change?

Happit: *playing* Reinstate more play in your life! It's surefire way to turn back you mental age clock. Borrow some kids if you have to in order to get in the mood. If you enjoyed playgrounds as a kid, find an adult version: a parcourse or fitness trail outfitted with fun exercise equipment along the way. How about a class in dancing with your dog, or training your dog for agility competitions? Have you heard of Frisbee golf? Buy a hula hoop! Or go into a big toy store and see what cool things kids have to choose from today. Get out and play catch with your kids. Borrow your daughter's scooter. Were you a Nancy Drew fan? Try geocaching, a fun activity that combines orienteering and detective work to find hidden prizes all over the world. Do this daily for those powerful, brain-training 21 days, then ask yourself how these activities might inform your vision for Your Big Happy Life.

Happit: *shining* Do something daily that uses your core talent. If you're stumped, ask other people what they think your core talent is. Rather than trying to get better at things you dislike, why not focus on what you excel at? How do you want to star in your life? Start a simple tracking system and make sure you do at least one thing daily for 21 days that engages your most significant talent. Extra credit if others see and notice you doing it, but it's really about spending your time in ways that *you* find fulfilling. *Work doesn't have to be work!*

Happit: *over-delivering* Find something every day that you can over-deliver on. It can be small and simple, like adding an index to a report or doing a deeper level of research. Or perhaps you cook a family meal without using any processed foods or sew Susie a sassy Halloween costume—without complaint. Maybe while house sitting for your neighbor you fill her house with flowers for her return. What can you do that's unexpected? How can you add value to your efforts? Would it be worth working half the night to blow your boss away with a snazzy promo video? If it's your usual M.O. to just kinda get by, to fly under the radar, this happit will change all that. **Adopting this happit gets you noticed in a big way**, and can increase your happiness level—IF you enjoy life in the spotlight. Go ahead and see what it's like to be that person who really excels big time. Then after you've tried it, see if it's an authentic fit. If not, that's okay too. Some people prefer a less intense approach to life. If you do enjoy it, then include it in your happy vision. Authenticity trumps everything. Build your happiness visions on the rock of who you really are, Commune with your best self, your highest self, your most authentic version of you. Display your true colors in all their vivid glory.

Happit: *enlarging* Just when you thought you were done creating you own vision, we challenge you to dream even BIGGER, to open up to the full rainbow of possibilities for Your Big Happy Life. Take every idea you have, no matter how tiny, examine it and find a way to make it even a little bit bigger—and when you can, make it a LOT bigger. (And bigger doesn't have to mean literally larger in size. Think regional not local; global not national; a deeper meaning, a greater value.) **Every day for the next 21 days find at least one way to expand your vision for Your Big Happy Life.** Imagine how much richer it will become in just three short weeks! A life is only as big as the dream you dare to live.

Happit: *affirming* You've undoubtedly heard the affirmation spiel before (and perhaps you've tried a version that didn't work for you). That's because **repeating intentions only helps if it inspires you to take ACTION on your desires**. That said, you *can* infuse your affirmation practice with extra oomph if you combine it with physicality, such as: saying—or shouting—them aloud; walking or running while you say them; do them to music and dance; say several sets of them while on a treadmill or bike. Mike does jumping jacks or cartwheels while shouting affirmations. Oriana says them aloud to Vivaldi every morning. **Write out a flock of affirmations using present tense, stating what you want as though you already have it.** Repeat them daily for—you guessed it—21 days straight (or curved) (or zigged) (or zagged). Examples:
- NOT: I'll be happy if I get a job at NASA. INSTEAD: I am happily employed as a Martian cartographer.
- NOT: I avoid all foods that are bad for me. INSTEAD: I am healthier than I've ever been, and I savor eating food that enhances my great health.
- NOT: I stop being depressed because I'm still single. INSTEAD: I love being in a nurturing relationship with a caring, sensitive partner.
- NOT: I no longer need to work 18-hour days. INSTEAD: I value my personal time, and I create a healthy balance between work and pleasure.
- NOT: I break my habit of obsessing all over eBay for vintage troll dolls. INSTEAD: I enjoy my troll collection and believe I have more than enough to enjoy them in every room of my house.

Happit: *previewing* For 21 days in a row, add new items to your Pinterest boards that represent Your Big Happy Life. **See how much emotion you can stir up and attach to them, which is a key to their effectiveness.** Believe in your dreams and they may come true; believe in yourself and they will come true.

Happit: *continuing* If you have a big project or goal you want to work toward as part of Your Big Happy Life, challenge yourself to put in some daily effort for each of those magical 21 days. Promise to devote 15 minutes minimally, as they are the toughest. After the first 15 minutes, you may well keep going and shock yourself how much you can do at oh:dark:thirty. After three weeks you'll be happitized to complete your project…and won't that feel good! To help you with this, you might make a **nag sign** for your mirror that not-so-gently nudges you to do one thing daily.

Happit: *beginning* On Day One make a list of OVER 21 new ways you could add joy to your life, then do one of them every day for 21 days. Why more than 21? Cuz some will be duds! If one tanks, pick another one, then you don't have an excuse to give up before you're done. (Some of you give up too easily, and we know who you are!) Whether you think you're ready or not, just start right now. There is magic in action.

Happit: *funning* We're both big list makers, and as with every other tip in this book, there are ways to do it with more joy. Use colored or patterned paper, bright pens, collaged images for inspiration—whatever will make you take notice (and action) when you see your list.
What would make it fun for you? **For those magical 21 days do some mundane thing in a radically big fun way.**
- Hauling the recycling to the curb? Rescue an item and upcycle it into something useful.
- Giving your dog a bath? Tint her pink with food coloring (doesn't work so well on black dogs!).
- Taking your car in for an oil change? Bring donuts for the crew (extreme ones with chocolate and sprinkles).
- Reviewing your fourth grader's book report? Help her illustrate it in living color. Or make a power point presentation about it. Or a music video.

Every single dull chore you do all day long CAN be made more fun. Do it for 21 days in a row and you'll do it forever. Now THAT'S a Big Happy Life!

Happit: *enduring* Stay in intimate contact with your irritant for 21 days and find creative ways to let it inspire your forward progress. For example, if your goal is to buy your first house and the irritant is living in cramped quarters surrounded by noisy neighbors, then really take that in. Note in your journal all the daily annoyances you endure. If your upstairs neighbor lifts clunky weights at 6 a.m., take out your earplugs and count how many times he drops his barbell on the floor above your bed. Use your anger to do whatever it takes to save the money to get the hell out of that Dodge. **If you just avoid or squelch your irritants, they can't help you.**

Happit: *spinning* Every day for the next 21 days look for something negative to turn upside down. (Even if some days you have to borrow someone else's sadness.) This is mostly a mental exercise, though it could also lead you to take action. **It can be trivial:** You break the heel off your ruby red pumps. *They hurt your feet because you bought them a half size too small, so good riddance!* **Or it may be a bigger deal:** You learn your brother needs a bone marrow transplant. *Which gives you a chance to step up and see if you're a match, which repairs an old rift between you.* It might only take a few seconds some days, or it may take an hour of soul searching on another. **The point is to not give up until you find the pearl...which is yours to keep.** You're welcome.

Happit: *applauding* **Create your own Box of Uplifts (or bag or cylinder or bucket) and add at least one accolade to it every day for those 21 all-important days.** This is quick to do and a deceptively simple tool, but one that can transform any gray day. Because everyone needs a boost now and then, delving into your Box of Uplifts will refocus your mind on what's true about you. **JOY-FILLED TWIST:** make one for someone you live with and add something new every day for 21 days, at which point let them take over. First you train your brain to remember how amazing this other person is—then you teach *them* to train their own brain to believe it! (A guaranteed relationship repair kit, at no extra charge!)

Happit: *flipping* **Monitor what comes out of your mouth daily for—you guessed it—21 days, and stop yourself from indulging in non-productive negative speak.** (Giving someone constructive criticism is fine; griping about your boss and his pet aardvark is not. Well, perhaps if the aardvark bites you.) Every time you catch yourself about to whine or gossip, flip it around and find something positive to say instead. Nothing comes to mind? Then say nuthin'. Granny was right: if you can't say something nice, don't say anything. This sort of mindless negative speak really reduces your happiness, and on some level it makes you feel bad, too, whether or not you consciously relate it to what just spewed out of your apple pie hole. Be sure to taste your words before you spit them out!

Happit: *optimizing* By now you know the plan: for the next 21 days **find some way to optimize happiness among people on your Joy Team**, whether at work, at home or any other place your desires lure you. It can a tiny gesture (picking up an extra latte or your way to the office) or a grand one (picking up the spirits of a friend who's just suffered a major loss). Just consciously do something every single day. No fair searching back over your day looking for actions that fit this happit—**you must be aware of your action as you are doing it**. It needs to be *intentional* for this to create a new neural pathway through that noggin of yours.

Happit: *declaring* Tell someone you love them for 21 days in a row. It might be your spouse, another family member or a friend—mix it up—*who* it is is less important than your saying it daily. No writing this time, the magic words must be spoken aloud, which is great practice for the shy and repressed (and you know who you are!).

Happit: *thanking* Once a day for…how long?…yep, 21 days, write someone a thank you note and mail it or hand deliver it. It must be in writing on actual paper, or bark, or perhaps in the sand if you've got a beach and a big stick. Want to go BIG? Hire a skywriter! Take out a personal ad. (No, a flippin' email doesn't count. Nor does a tweet or a poke or a pin. Pick up a pen before you forget how!) Bonus points if you thank 21 different people. No fair thanking the same person over and over for the same thing, no matter how grateful you are for the shiny new kidney. Well, maybe that's the exception that breaks the rule.

www.ingramcontent.com/pod-product-compliance
Lightning Source LLC
Chambersburg PA
CBHW080441170426
43195CB00017B/2845